Shattered Dreams of a Runaway Nun

Grace Lux Dunford

with Gerty Shipmaker

SHATTERED DREAMS OF A RUNAWAY NUN
Copyright © 2013 by Grace Lux Dunford
with Gerty Shipmaker

ISBN: 978-1-77069-766-9

Printed in Canada

Word Alive Press
131 Cordite Road, Winnipeg, MB R3W 1S1
www.wordalivepress.ca

Library and Archives Canada Cataloguing in Publication
Dunford, Grace, 1935-
    Shattered dreams of a runaway nun / Grace Dunford
with Gerty Shipmaker.
ISBN 978-1-77069-766-9

    1. Dunford, Grace, 1935-. 2. Ex-nuns--Saskatchewan--Biography.
3. Self-realization--Religious aspects--Christianity. 4. Catholic women--
Biography. 5. Spiritual life--Catholic Church. I. Shipmaker, Gerty, 1960-
II. Title.
BX4705.D8682A3 2012   282.092   C2012-907552-3

This is my story
This is my song;
Praising my Saviour all day long.

To the all-loving and faithful Saviour, Jesus,
His wonderful, ever present Father,
and to the patient Holy Spirit,
I dedicate this work.

ACKNOWLEDGEMENTS

Many people have been involved with this book. These are just a few who helped along the way.

I would like to thank my sister, Ann, who actually started me on this journey.

Thank you to my nephews, Tim Zerr and Bruce Weicker for their encouragement.

To Carol Waugh who was courageous enough to plow through the first draft. And to someone who has become a very good friend and someone who understands me better than I ever thought possible - Gerty Shipmaker. She took the facts and put emotions into them. Thank you for the hours and hours of hard work.

But most of all I want to thank my husband Ivan, who put up with my mood swings as I battled through things I had never dealt with before.

Whatever becomes of this book, I thank God for all He has seen me through over the years. May His name be forever praised.

Grace Dunford
March 2013

PROLOGUE:
To a Deserted Island

*A man's mind plans his way, but the Lord directs his steps
and makes them sure.*
Proverbs 16:9

It is six o'clock of an August evening when we begin our journey to a deserted island. The sky is clear; the air calm. Everything we might ever need has been safely stowed below, and as I stand on the deck of our twenty-seven-foot sailboat, the *Cantata*, with the man I love beside me, I feel the excitement of a dream about to be realized.

We are three days from sailing the open seas, three hours from our last stop before quite literally leaving everything and everyone behind us. There is only one thing left to do, and that is to have our boat lifted out of the water to be inspected and to fix a leak between the hull and the keel. To that end, Bob starts the small motor and we head south.

Together we sit on the deck, enjoying the warm evening, silent in our excitement, almost not believing that we have made it this far. Everything is finally going according to the plans that have been in the works for months, and we relax. In three days we will be completely alone to sail the seas, eventually to land on the deserted tropical island of Suverov to live in isolation together.

I look at Bob and can't help but smile. The beard he's been growing looks good on him; he looks like a hippy, and it matches his soul. I'm so proud to be with him on this journey, to be his wife, even if only common-law. I close my eyes as the boat gently skims the water.

When we feel a slight breeze begin, we turn our faces to it and inhale the pleasant smell of the water. We need no words to acknowledge that we were born for this time and this place.

As the minutes tick by, our silent contentment is broken as the breeze gives way to a good wind. Bob and I look at each other, knowing there had been no storms in the forecast. We realize that we still have almost two hours to our destination, and we sit up and take notice.

None of our sails are up, and in fact all but the jib are stored below. With only clear skies in the forecast, we are making the trip with just our small motor. We are ill-equipped to face a storm, and as the sky darkens we each begin a personal journey of worry.

The wind doesn't let up; in fact, it starts to howl as if to warn us about what lies ahead. The water begins to boil in agreement with the wind. Bob tries to raise the jib, which will help us navigate the storm, but he is struggling. I watch as he tries over and over to fight the gales. He finally gives up, as the weather is simply too rough to raise it. Left with just the motor for navigation, he has his hands full.

It seems as if we are going straight from calm to hell. I tremble as the waves get bigger and the boat tips at their mercy. Without sails, it becomes apparent that we are now controlled by the storm, going wherever it takes us. When our boat starts heaving back and forth, pitched by the waves, Bob doesn't give up trying to gain some measure of control. He concentrates fully on the task at hand. I can't tell if he's gaining any control at all, and I desperately want to ask him if he thinks we'll be okay, but I stay silent, too fearful of his answer to even ask.

Just as I'm wondering where the best place is for me to be, I hear Bob's voice over the wind. "Check down below! See that we're not taking on water!"

I had momentarily forgotten that we're sailing a vessel that has a leak; it had seemed so minor when we left Frenchman's Creek in the sunlight only an hour earlier. Now I understand the impact of what we might be facing and hurry down the stairs to the cabin below. With horror I stare at the front of the cabin; with the water churning and slamming against the hull, the leak we are mere hours from fixing is now letting water in. It isn't rushing in, but I know I need a plan to remove it. I find a small pail that I can use to bail with.

Before tackling the water, I go back above. The rain has started, adding even more misery to an already grim situation. Bob is now fighting eight-foot waves, and I begin to wonder if we'll even make it to Nanaimo, our first stop. Not daring to get close enough to the sides to hold on to the ropes, I stand at the top of the hatch and yell out to him, letting him know about the situation below.

Whether or not he hears me above the howling wind I don't know, because my stomach, always a little weak, can no longer take the wild movements of the boat. My focus becomes hurrying back down the stairs to let my stomach empty itself.

I have to lie down for a while, as the nausea I'm feeling is accompanied by strong stomach pains. While I've experienced similar pain in the past, I'm chalking this all up to the rough water, even though I have never before suffered from seasickness. Rest is almost impossible as I see the water seeping in, and so I take the pail, scoop up some water, go up the stairs, and hang on while I throw the water back where it came from.

Back down the stairs, I throw up again and have to lie down. The pain in my stomach isn't stopping. Meanwhile, Bob is struggling against the storm, hanging on to the motor and wildly hoping it will aid in directing us where we want to go.

As the sea spills its anger towards us, some of the waves crash over the stern, and water goes down the hatch and into the cabin. I know I can't close the hatch because I need the access to bail water. Each time I go up, the storm seems as furious as before. I look out over the water at the raging, violent swells and am overwhelmed by the fact that I might end up in that darkness.

I can't swim.

I am absolutely and thoroughly terrified. I try to throw out a few words to the God I have tried to know all my life, but I'm convinced he's not going to hear me. I wonder if I've lived for thirty-six years only to come to an end here. I spend a moment listing all the other dreams that I've had and watched shatter to pieces. It doesn't take much for the tears to come.

I let them fall, but only for a few moments, because I know that until I'm in the water I'm going to fight for this particular dream. It matters too much to me. So I pick up my pail and continue to fight back.

By 9 p.m. it's dark and we have to rely on our charts to navigate. Neither Bob nor I had worried too much about our old charts for this leg of our journey because our plan was to arrive in daylight. Now in the darkness I'm not so sure how Bob will find the harbour.

When harbour lights appear, our relief is palpable. I feel like I've faced death and conquered it. Even with the storm still raging, there is hope in those lights.

Our jubilation disappears when we realize that the lights we see are different from our chart. We cannot take a chance on hitting any rocks. We have no choice but to turn around. My heart sinks, and the fear takes over with a vengeance. Now we are at the complete mercy of the wind.

If it's at all possible, my fear intensifies. It begins to choke me. I have no idea where we're going, no idea where we'll end up. We have no relevant charts, as we were headed south and now are headed north.

The night grows long and we grow weary. I feel weak from my constant vomiting and bailing. *Cantata* continues to lurch along, allowing the storm to bend it to its will, first one way, then back again. It doesn't let up. I cry out to God again, but my words just fall on what I presume are deaf ears.

By the time daylight arrives, we are exhausted but thankful to be alive. It appears that the storm is lessening, yet we are still running in front of it, hoping it will be gentle as it finds our landing place for us.

All day we are thrown along by the water, waiting as the storm slowly subsides and eventually stops altogether.

At 3 p.m. we are grateful to recognize our surroundings, finding ourselves at Tribune Bay on Hornby Island, much farther north than we originally set out to go. Without charts for this area, we have to rely on what we see, and what we see is the bottom of the bay made up of flat rocks. Flat rocks make it very difficult to set the anchors, and after fighting the storm all night and day we aren't exactly at our peak. The adrenaline of being alive pushes us to struggle together until our anchors take hold, and our ordeal is over for now.

In somewhat of a state of shock, we go below deck. I suggest a cup of tea to Bob, and he groggily agrees. As I put the water on to boil, we talk about what we have just overcome. We don't take it lightly that our lives have been spared, that we have just come through a harrowing twenty-one hours.

We have just begun to talk about what we will do next when we hear voices. Going up we look toward the shore and see a group of people waving to us, offering us their home to dry out. They look like angels to me, and I eagerly turn off the water for our tea and join Bob to let the dinghy off the boat and go to dry land.

Sitting in the home of our newly found friends, we regale them with our adventure. It is starting to feel surreal, all that we have just come through, and talking about it renews my gratitude to be alive. I feel even more alive now, having survived what we did, and though short on sleep I am excited to continue our dream.

While drinking the most delicious cup of tea I've ever tasted, relieved to be on dry ground, I glance out the window towards the bay. I cannot believe what I'm seeing.

"Bob! The boat! Our boat! It's moving!"

As one we all jump up and go to the window and watch as *Cantata* starts swinging around. We don't stop to think as we all rush to grab our jackets and run out the door and down to the bay. We get there just in time to see *Cantata* going before the wind, heading for shore.

It becomes obvious that the kedge anchor has cut loose, and as it swings around, the main anchor also slips free of the rocks. We stand helpless on the shore as we watch it drift off.

Straight towards the rocks.

With morbid fascination I stare and watch it move in slow motion. After all we've been through in the last twenty-four hours, it doesn't seem possible that I'm watching our boat drift towards potential destruction.

I hold my breath as it inches even closer, as if my breathless state has the power to keep it upright and unharmed. But it's no use.

It is almost more than I can bear, watching as it crashes against the rocks and falls over onto its side. I fall down right where I am and begin to cry.

My dream. Our dream. Our future. It all lies shattered against the rocks. Just like so many before it.

I can't bear to look any more. I put my head down and sob.

The First Day

My beloved speaks and says to me, Rise up, my love,
my fair one, and come away.
Song of Solomon 2:10

It didn't take very much to get me out of bed that morning. It was September 4, 1953. I awoke early in anticipation, knowing that my life was going to be radically altered from this day on. I would be taking drastic but exciting steps in fulfilling my destiny, continuing on the path that had been set before me from perhaps the day I was born.

That day was my eighteenth birthday, and I had been focused on it for a very long time. While other girls my age were beginning careers, continuing schooling, or even planning a life of marriage and babies, I was choosing a different path, and I couldn't wait.

I looked around the room, my bedroom since I was ten years old. I had decorated it myself; it was my space, my place of comfort, and I knew that in all likelihood I would never see it again. But I was eager to get my life going, eager to leave the family home, my childhood, the turbulent relationship I had with my dad. I jumped out of bed, ready to leave it all behind.

I wasn't quite as eager to leave my mom, however, and there was sadness when I thought of that separation. I was the youngest of her thirteen children, and we had a very close relationship. I was used to being apart from her for months at a time, as I had already been in boarding school for four years, but I knew this time would be different. From this day on I wouldn't be able to phone her when I was lonely or just wanted to chat. I wouldn't be able to hop on the train and be home within the hour. This separation would be much more permanent.

I couldn't allow my thoughts to dwell on life without my mother a constant in it. The thought of only being able to see her once a year for a brief visit was more than I could handle emotionally, so I busied myself with focusing on what the day would bring. I checked and rechecked the things I had packed against the list I had been given, making sure I had the required stockings, shoes, undergarments, nightgowns, towels, sheets, and of course my Sunday dress. I would be wearing the only other dress needed, my everyday one. The thought that these two dresses would be my entire wardrobe for the next year was a little daunting, but I knew it wouldn't matter to me once my new life began.

There wasn't much left to pack, but I had to be sure that nothing was missing. As I closed my case for the last time I knew I couldn't really know what the rest of my life would look like, but I had a pretty good idea, and I couldn't wait to head down the stairs and out the door.

With everything packed, my bed made, and my room clean, I turned my attention to getting dressed. I took the garment that I had made myself with the fabric and pattern I had been given and pulled it over my head. As the black serge fell crisply around my body, the reality of this day overwhelmed me. By day's end my life as I knew it would be over and I would begin fulfilling my destiny, my dream.

That day, my eighteenth birthday, I would become a nun.

I knew it would be a six-year journey before I would make my final vows, but entering the convent, wearing the clothes, saying the prayers, meditating, following the regimented schedule, and singing the beautiful music had me giddy with anticipation. I couldn't wait to get started.

I had always known that I was to be a nun. I'm not sure why I was the one who was chosen to be a nun and not any of my five older sisters, but that was the way it was, and I embraced it wholeheartedly. I had tried to get into the convent back in grade 9, when I was only fourteen, but Mother Superior suggested I wait until after I completed high school. During those years of waiting while I was in St. Ursula's Academy I watched the nuns dreamily as I thought of the day when I would become one of them.

In any Roman Catholic family, having a nun or priest among the children was one of the highest honours, and for me to carry that honour for my family was a privilege. Entering into a life of poverty, chastity, and obedience was not something I was doing only because it was expected, however. I truly wanted that life for myself.

You might say that I had a teenage crush on Jesus. My dream was to have a relationship with him where we could talk and he would be with me all the time. Becoming a bride of Christ was the only way I saw of entering into that relationship.

I had read many books about the lives of saints, and I wanted to be just like them. Even though I was from a large family, I always felt different from everyone else, the odd man out. There was a constant loneliness within me, and I expected that Jesus would fill that loneliness when I became his bride. I would do all that was required of me, and I knew that he would reward me with his presence.

As I looked down at my new clothing, my simple dress, I knew it would forever separate me from the fashions that all my friends would be wearing. Even though I willingly wore this dress, I knew what I would be giving up. I loved fashion and had spent many happy hours creating costumes from wonderful fabrics throughout my high school years. I shrugged off what could have become a negative moment, picked up my suitcase, and with one last look around my childhood bedroom, I headed down the stairs.

There was no grand farewell. Being the youngest child by five years, I was now the only one left at home, so there were no siblings to wish me well. We were a big family and one that didn't stand on emotional ceremony; my leave-taking was a non-event. Two weeks earlier we had taken a family photo, and that was as good as any goodbye. Besides, I'd been away for much of the past four years, so it wasn't nearly as big a change for them as it was for me. I was far too thrilled to be finally entering the convent to think about the lack of goodbyes.

It was a thirty-minute drive from Humboldt, Saskatchewan, to the small community of Bruno where the convent was located. It was a familiar road, as I'd traveled it often to and from boarding school.

As we drove up the drive, past the beautiful gardens that the nuns tended, I looked at the building where I'd spent my high school years and at the new addition recently completed, the place that had been closed to me and the other students. The closest we came to the life behind those doors was joining the nuns in chapel for Mass and prayers. Now I would be among the privileged, a postulant, a first-year nun. I wanted to hurry out of the car and run into that building, I was that excited.

My parents and I calmly and quietly entered the convent and were led to one of the two parlours, where we would wait until the nuns came to get me for the official ceremony. There was one other girl entering, Delores. We went to high school together, and she was in the second parlour with her family.

This was the time for me to say goodbye to my mother and father. Because of my excitement and their approval, there were no tears, no sadness, just a simple goodbye as if we'd see each other again in a week or so.

When the time came, we entered the chapel. My parents sat in the back row and watched as I received the white headband with a short black veil and the white collar of a postulant. At this stage of my training, I was allowed to let my hair show under my veil, but only until I became a novice, which would happen the following May.

Delores and I were asked very solemnly if our desire was to enter the Ursuline order. With all my heart I replied, "Yes." Before we knew it, the ceremony was over, and we were led out of the chapel.

I felt euphoric. I had done it! I was officially a nun!

As I was led into the halls where only the brides and future brides of Christ could go, I wanted to pinch myself. It was hard to take it all in, and I had the feeling of walking on holy ground.

One of the Sisters, a novice, was assigned to me to help me learn all I needed to know, and she took me downstairs to the dining hall. Coffee was being served, and I was welcomed into the order by the other

Sisters. From there I was shown the novitiate, the room where classes were held, and given a locker for my belongings and my own prayer books. With those in hand we went straight to chapel for afternoon Office and meditation before dinner.

In the chapel for the first time as a nun, I sat in wonder. It was as if I were a flower in the warmth of the sun, ready to bloom. I didn't mind for a second that the Office prayers were recited in Latin and I couldn't understand a word or join in. All I could do was bask in my new relationship with Jesus. I couldn't wait to get to know him.

After a few moments, I opened my prayer book to attempt to follow along. I was happy to find an English translation on the opposite page, so I could understand the meaning of the prayers. When I opened my community prayer book, I saw that it was all in German with no translation. I was content to just sit back and listen. There I was in the company of a group of women all dedicated to the same purpose, Jesus, their beautiful voices lifted together in prayer. It was a thrill just to be among them, and I eagerly anticipated the day when my voice would be one with theirs.

After our evening meal Delores and I had an hour of recreation before night prayers. As this was our first evening, our task was to embroider the number we were assigned onto every piece of fabric we owned, from our stockings to our towels. I was most annoyed to find that I had been given the number eighty-three, and if that wasn't bad enough, I watched as Delores easily embroidered the number seventy-seven on her things.

Following night prayers it was time for bed, and I was led to my new sleeping quarters. I would be joining several other nuns (all in their early years of training) in a dorm room with the same layout as the school dorms where I had spent the last four years.

As I approached my bed on this first night as a nun, I saw that it was covered with flowers and notes of encouragement and welcome from the Sisters. It was such a wonderful surprise, giving a warm, wonderful feeling of being embraced into a new family. By this time we had officially entered into the Great Silence, the time where not a word was to be spoken. It began after night prayers and wasn't to be broken until the following morning after Mass. All I could do was smile a thank-you to all the faces around me. They were now my family.

My first day as a nun had ended. My heart was full of expectancy for the years ahead, but the events of the future were still very far away. Right now I was basking in the wonder of this day, certain that this was my calling, where I was to be, free to love the Lord and live for him.

If someone had told me then that in eleven years I would find myself walking through dark halls to the farthest doorway of the convent in the middle of the night, running to get away, I would have laughed at them.

I was that sure of my life.

Fearfully and Wonderfully Made

*Your eyes saw my unformed substance, and in Your book all the
days [of my life] were written before ever they took shape,
when as yet there was none of them.*
Psalm 139:16

There are many factors in the making of a person, not only to their
physical making but, more importantly, the essence of a person:
their character, their core. Who I was (and am), why I made the choices I
did, how I came to struggle with so many issues, all are deeply connected
with not only my own history but also the history of my parents and
the land where I was born. Had I been born in a different place, at a
different time and to a different family, I wouldn't be me.

But I am me, fearfully and wonderfully made.

My story actually begins in another land, in another time and
another way of life, foreign to us here in Canada in the 21st century.
My family's history is very closely entwined with the history of the part
of Saskatchewan where I was born. Many years before my birth, events
were being orchestrated on two continents and in two families that
would eventually come together to create my personal history.

Both my father, born in 1888, and my mother, born in 1891, were
from Austria-Hungary. Their villages were separated by twenty miles,
yet they knew nothing of each other. Austria-Hungary was ruled by

Emperor Francis Joseph I from the Hapsburg family, the traditional rulers of Austria. His empire was of the time and era where the people were defined by their different classes.

My father's family were serfs under the rule of a lord (the "graff") while my mother's family were landowners, putting them a little higher in the hierarchy. As part of the serfdom, my father's lot in life as a young man was to serve in the lord's army to fight for the emperor.

It was 1903, and both my father and his cousin were facing the time when they would be called to serve and fight. Their fathers, wanting a better future for their sons, devised a daring plan to get the boys out of the country. Between them they had barely enough money to get the boys smuggled out of the country in a hay cart and to buy a berth on a ship headed for North America.

My father was fourteen years old when he landed in New York at Ellis Island, and he and his cousin had just eighteen pennies between them. They knew they were to go from New York to Minnesota, where they had relatives and were promised work on the railroad, but they had no idea how to get there. This was as far at their fathers' money got them; from here on in they were on their own.

There they were, two young men, boys, really, in a strange country. With almost no money, no understanding of the language and no ideas, so far away from their family and any familiarity, they faced the first of many challenges their new land would give them. Having passed through all the inspections required of immigrants to the United States of America, they were left to wait in a long room, sitting on benches with all the others. As the hours went by, the room grew emptier and emptier until only the two of them were left.

I can only imagine what they had been expecting and how it compared to their new reality. What must it have been like for them to be sitting there all alone, knowing that they likely didn't have enough money to go farther? Did they try to decide together what they should do next, or did they just sit quietly waiting? What were they waiting for? Did they wonder what their pennies would buy in this strange land and whether they should they spend them on food? Did they try to communicate with anyone? Did they plan to sleep there in the waiting room? Did my father question his own father's decision to take him away from all that was familiar? Was he disappointed that he wouldn't get the chance to fight for his country? Or was he was grateful to be given a new start?

I never asked him those questions, and he never volunteered any information, so I can only guess at what he endured and how he felt, knowing that he might never see his family again, thrust into a country likely not of his own choosing. I am sure the experience changed who he was and formed who he became as a man, a husband and a father.

Finally, a woman they had never seen before approached them and began talking to them in a form of their mother tongue. Taking stock of the situation, she gave them a basket of food and put them on the train to Minnesota.

While my father was being smuggled out of his homeland, his future was being prepared for him in Canada.

Canada at the turn of the twentieth century was still a rugged country. There were vast uninhabited spaces, and western Canada in particular was calling out for immigrants. In 1865, the Canadian Pacific Railway had cut across southern Saskatchewan (then known as the North-Western Territories), and land became available for homesteaders. In the northern United States the land was already settled up to the Canadian border, and many German settlers from the closest states began moving north into Canada, welcoming the opportunity for obtaining land. Many of those were from Minnesota.

As those settlers began the arduous task of earning their land, they saw great opportunities and began sending requests back to their parishes in the States for more immigrants to found new colonies. One of those requests was received by the abbot of St. John's Abbey in Collegeville, Minnesota, a large German Catholic colony. He was persuaded to establish a similar colony in Saskatchewan. In 1902 he sent an exploration party to Canada, headed up by Reverend Bruno Doerfler. The party's mission was to explore a suitable location for a colony centred on a Benedictine monastery.

As a result of this exploration, the decision to establish the colony was made, and the Volksverein German-American Land Company was founded. In 1902, together with the priests of the Order of St. Benedict and the Catholic Settlement Society of St. Paul, Minnesota, this company was given the rights to colonize a vast area in north-central Saskatchewan. The German-American Land Company was responsible for buying and selling 100,000 acres of railroad land to settlers. The priests' role was to develop parishes and expand the settlement.

Bruno and a handful of families immigrated to Saskatchewan at this time and by 1903, St. Peter's Colony was established with the help of the Benedictine monks from Illinois and Collegeville. By the end of that year, over a thousand homesteads had been filed and eight parishes established.

My father was one of those homesteaders. Within a year of his arrival in North America, he too had heard of land available in Canada. He had discovered that he didn't enjoy working for someone else, so he joined those headed to Saskatchewan. He took a homestead in St. Peter's Colony around what is now the village of Carmel. Barely sixteen years old, he worked long hours trying to get some results from that rocky, hard land. It was back-breaking work and very unsatisfying.

Within a few years he moved from this land, finding it unforgiving. He began again on a new homestead seven miles to the east, two and a half miles from a tiny settlement called Dixon. Dixon consisted of only a one-room schoolhouse, some grain elevators, and a few houses for the schoolteacher and the elevator operators. It was about five miles west of Humboldt, which had become the centre of St. Peter's Colony.

The land on Dad's new homestead was much richer and prospered under his care. Dad eventually expanded this farm to seven and a half quarters.

At the same time that my father was being smuggled out of his homeland and adjusting to a foreign life, my mother's family was also undergoing changes. As land owners in Austria-Hungary they had some money, so their lives were somewhat better than my father's. My mother would tell me stories of raising silkworms and picking mulberry leaves to feed them. Her family also grew flax, and she spoke of beating the flax to free the fibres to spin the cloth. Her stories would mesmerize me as a young girl.

When my mother was just two years old, in 1893, she and her older brother were playing with some pieces of glass, pressing them against their eyes, pretending they were eyeglasses. She tripped and fell, causing the glass to cut into her eye. There was nothing the doctors could do but remove the eye. Yet it didn't keep her from doing anything. Growing up, it was not something we even thought about, as she didn't let it prevent her from doing or experiencing anything.

My mother's father moved his family to a homestead in St. Peter's Colony in 1903, the same year my father came to North America. In 1907 my mother's own mother passed away, and within two years Mom was running the household for her father and four younger brothers, the task falling to her automatically when her older sister married.

As long as my mother could remember she had wanted to be a nun, but all that changed one evening in 1909 during a snowstorm. There was a sudden knock at the door, and there stood my father. He had become lost in the storm and felt quite relieved when he saw the light in the window of their farmhouse.

He was immediately welcomed and ushered into the home. As he stepped inside, my mother heard a quiet voice within her tell her, "This is the man you are going to marry." Needless to say, she was not at all happy to hear that, as her heart was set on becoming a nun, but the decision to marry was not up to her. Within a few months her father had arranged a marriage between the two, and knowing that her father's word was law, there was no choice for her but to be married.

They were married on January 18, 1910. He was twenty-one years old, she just eighteen. They loaded all her possessions on a wagon, including a few chickens in a crate, tied a milk cow behind the wagon, and off they went to the farm, where my father had built a sod house. My parents lived there until my father built them a proper house, and in 1922 that became a chicken coop when a three-storey brick home was built.

This homestead and this home is where I was born and where we lived until I was ten years old.

Homesteading on the Prairies

Ask of Me, and I will give You the nations as Your inheritance,
and the uttermost parts of the earth as Your possession.
Psalm 2:8

By the time she was pregnant with me, my mother had already birthed twelve children. One of them, a son, had passed away as a young child. Her youngest was five years old when Mom found out she was pregnant with me. She was forty-three years old. From what I've heard within the family, my father was none too pleased that there would be another child, and my arrival in the middle of harvesting season only made my impending birth more negative.

Harvesting season on a large farm in Saskatchewan was a busy time. My father would have had up to fifteen men waiting to be directed and kept on task. When Mom went into labour on one of those busy days, Dad ranted and raved as he drove her to the hospital. While it was only a fifteen-mile round trip, it was time he felt he could ill afford and would cost him money.

To make matters even worse for my father, I was a girl, so there wasn't even the relief that there would be an extra hand on the farm as the years went by. I was just another mouth to feed.

Dad's relationship with his children was rocky at best. He tended to play favourites, and I'm told that my sister Magdalene was his most favoured. I think Emma was a pretty close second, because when she talks about her relationship with Dad, it is very different from anything I ever had. The boys had their own unique relationship with him. All but one had to have a major fight with him in order to gain freedom from his domination.

It was no secret in the family that I wasn't welcomed by my dad, and it was evidenced by our relationship. He rarely spoke to me growing up, trying to forget I existed, and never showed me any love.

As difficult as my relationship with my father was, I had a very special bond with my mother. Perhaps it was because I was her youngest or the only girl of her last five children, or maybe she was making up for the lack of love from my father, but whatever the reason, our relationship was unique. We were very close. The best times were when we were alone at home when I was just a little girl. I don't know where my father went, but when he was gone I would be allowed to sleep in Mom's bed. She would make me "milk soup," hot sweetened milk and toast, the best thing in the world to me!

My mother amazed me with her talents. Even with her limited vision she could sew any piece of clothing by just looking at a picture of it. She made curtains, painted walls with her own borders around the ceilings in place of mouldings, crocheted amazing doilies, was a gourmet cook, and had quite the green thumb, both with house plants and in the garden.

Her garden was a small farm of its own. It took almost three acres of land to grow the food needed to keep our family and hired hands fed. Keeping the garden watered was no easy task in the days before sprinkling systems. Our water had to be hauled in barrels on a stone boat, a flat bottomed sled on two steel runners that was pulled by a team of horses. Then it had to be dipped out of the barrels and poured around each plant, a job that fell to us children. It wasn't easy, but we preferred it to weeding that large garden.

The most important ingredient in my mother's character was her relationship with Jesus. She put her faith in him and wanted to serve him as best she could. Although circumstances never allowed her to be a nun, she walked very close to him. In fact, he appeared to her twice when she was very ill and healed her both times. Later on when we moved off the farm and into town, she and I would attend Mass together every day before breakfast. It was her example of living with Jesus that pulled me even closer towards being a nun.

The homestead where I spent my early childhood was a magnificent place for a child to grow up. I loved so many things there, from the farming aspect to life in our home. There was never a dull moment for me, and my childhood was idyllic.

On occasion our family would venture off the homestead to go somewhere together in the car. Mom and Dad sat in the front, and the kids piled in the back. On one trip when I was four years old, as usual I was sitting on one of my brothers' laps in the back seat. This was well before any seatbelts were even found in a car! I was holding on to the door handle to keep my balance as we bumped over the country roads when there was a shift. I felt the door give way under my hand. Before I knew it I was hanging on the outside of the moving car.

I distinctly remember thinking that if I let go they wouldn't even know I was gone and I would be left behind, so I hung on for dear life. It took Dad the length of an entire city block to realize what had happened and to stop the car. My knees were all skinned up, but there was nothing broken, so back in the car I went, and we carried on with our trip.

Life on the farm centred around our home. I loved our three-storey 1922 brick farmhouse. There was no electricity yet in our neck of the woods, so my brothers devised a system to bring lights into our home. Somehow they managed to acquire fifty or more car batteries and housed them all on one wall in our basement. The batteries were hooked up to power our lights. When any of them would run low, they were brought outside and hooked up to the windmill in the yard to recharge. How they kept track of each battery and its charge I have no idea, but we sure enjoyed having lights.

The front of our house had a large screened-in porch, and through that was the seldom used front door, which opened into the parlour. Sometimes during the hot summer months we would have our meals in the porch, outside yet safe from all the bugs. This part of the house held its own magic, as special things happened there. The parlour, with its glorious stained glass window above a larger window that brought the daylight in, always held Christmas. Christmas was the only time we used it, when the tree was put up, and Dad would have his annual rest there in the afternoon of Christmas Eve. When the presents appeared under the tree to be opened that evening, I couldn't understand how he could have slept through Santa Claus bringing them.

Since the parlour wasn't used on a regular basis, there was no need to heat it, so the door to the dining room was kept closed most of the time. On the dining room side of that door was a three-foot-square heat register that brought the heat up from the coal furnace in the basement. Many cold winter evenings would find us huddled around that register. The large dining room had a huge table that could hold sixteen people for a meal. Many, many times there wasn't an empty chair around that table, especially during harvest time.

Off the dining room was the kitchen. Although not very large, it was the heart of the house. This is where most people entered the house, rather than using the front door. My mother had a beautiful stove in the kitchen with a warming closet and a hot water reservoir. As was common in that day, it was fuelled by wood. The wood box had to be kept filled at all times.

There was no running water into our home, so water was pumped from a cistern below the kitchen. That cistern had to be cleaned out once a year. Since I was the smallest, that became my job. There was no magic under the kitchen, let me tell you!

Mom and Dad's bedroom completed the ground floor. Between the kitchen and their bedroom was the hall, with stairs going down to the basement and to the upper floor. Upstairs were four bedrooms and a small room that my dad had built to eventually house a bathroom whenever running water would be available (that never did happen while we lived there).

From that floor was a staircase to the attic, full of treasures that opened up all sorts of creative possibilities to me. There were boxes upon boxes of wonderful old clothes that I would love trying on, one even containing my mother's wedding dress and veil.

The girls' bedroom had the only door that led out to a balcony above the front porch. When I was seven or eight years old, the last of my sisters moved out, and that room became mine, and the balcony became my stage. I don't know where the idea of performing came from, but there I first felt the pull to drama, music, costuming, and all that was involved with the stage. I composed my own music and created my own operas. With the treasures I found in the attic I put on what I thought were amazing performances to an audience of one—my mom. This passion for music and drama was only beginning.

Those years on the farm were busy. There were cows to be milked, a garden to be tended, spring planting, summer field work, and fall harvesting to be done. I didn't care for all the work—especially milking one particular cow, Carrot, who had hard teats—but I didn't shy away from helping. As a little girl I would love to get up at 5 a.m. and go out to the fields with my brothers. In the springtime they would let me sit on their laps and "drive" the tractors.

The lazy days of summer, before harvesting time, were long, warm, and wonderful. Of course there were still chores, but there was always time for playing. Our wash line hung from four posts in the ground, and on the south end between the posts there was a swing for us to play on. It was a typical swing with ropes and a plank for a seat, and I would spend hours there, swinging so hard I would get it to go all the way around. It was exhilarating!

It was 1939, and my favourite time of the year had arrived—harvesting season. The day was hot, the smell in the air was different, and I could feel the excitement. As soon as the dew was off the ground, the men in the family and the hired hands headed out to the fields with the tractor, thresher, grain box, and wagon. They set up everything ready to go and then came back to the house, where my mom, my sisters, and I had breakfast ready.

The large table was full of hungry men, not a chair empty. Talk was all about the day: the wheat, the machinery, the weather. It was jovial, full of expectancy. I loved sitting and listening to the men talk, just breathing in and feeling all their excitement.

After the hearty meal the men headed back to the fields, this time to stay until the day's work was done. I went off with them, fully planning on working as hard as any of them. I prayed that today's trip to the granary would include two teams and wagons, because then I might be allowed to drive one of them by myself all the way to Dixon, a whole two and a half miles. That would make for a perfect day, I thought, as I headed out the door without even a goodbye to my mother.

I was fairly bouncing as I reached the section of the field where we would be working. As usual, the tractor was in front of the thresher, and as one of the boys started her up the noise of the day began. A wide belt from the power drive on the tractor went to a wheel on the threshing machine, and as the tractor started, the thresher was also cranked up and ready to go. What a wonderful riotous noise those machines made!

Some of the boys had already gone farther into the fields to bring the stooks in. Stooks are the sheaves of wheat stacked together after cutting and binding, ready to be fed into the thresher. Other workers were waiting to throw them onto the feeding belt, which would take them into the body of the machine, where the grain would be beaten out and separated from the straw. The straw would be blown out, and the grain would go through the hopper into the grain box.

Once the process was in motion, my job began. I was lifted high into the grain box next to the hopper. The box sat on stilts, giving me a great view of what was happening around me. But I didn't have much time to look, as the grain began to come through the hopper and fall around me. I quickly moved it as it fell into the box, making sure it was placed evenly in the box. I worked hard pushing the grain into the corners, then the sides, and then to the middle. I was positive that it was the most important job out there.

After a few hours it was time to shut off the machine and take a break, as my mom and sisters had arrived with lunch. While I had been working with the men, the women had been busy in the house preparing food for us all. Now they laid out the big pots of food and iced drinks. I was excited to take a break because we all stopped working and ate together. Every day at this time we had what I called a picnic, and everyone relaxed in the quiet of the midday. I didn't think life could get any better.

It was hot getting back to work after lunch, but I felt refreshed, knowing that the best was yet to come. As the threshing went on, the grain was eventually poured from my box through a trap door into a wagon below it. I watched eagerly as the wagon filled up and a second was brought in. When I saw the second one reaching its capacity I knew it was time for a trip to the granary. I waited anxiously to see if I would be given the privilege of driving one of the teams of horses with a wagonload of grain.

It was my lucky day, and I was allowed to go. I climbed up behind the team, feeling strong, important, grown-up, and completely in charge. The reality was that the horses were in charge of me, knowing the way to the granary as well as, if not better, than me, but, at five years old, I didn't see that at all. All I knew was this was the highlight of the season for me, driving the team all the way to Dixon, a five-mile round trip.

When I came back from the granary, however, I knew the day for this five-year-old was done, and I went back inside the house. It had been a fantastic day and one I hoped I would able to repeat.

Sundays on the farm were great days, no matter what time of year it was. We would all go to church, by car in the summer or by horse and sleigh in the winter, and the house would usually fill up with company for a large dinner after church. It seemed like our farm was a desired place to be on a Sunday afternoon. In the summer the boys would play baseball and the adults would visit. One thing was for sure: there was never any work done on the Sabbath day.

Dad was extremely hard-working and demanded the same of his children. He started out breaking the land with a team of oxen (remember, he was only sixteen years old at the time), walking behind the plough, eventually clearing the largest portion of the seven and a half quarters of land himself.

As the years went on, he became involved with the growing of new grains for the university, which led him to selling Elephant Brand fertilizer and then starting a farm equipment dealership for Minneapolis-Moline and Oliver Tractors. Then he started a car dealership, for Kaiser-Frazer cars and then for Buick and Plymouth, called Lux Agencies, which at one time had three outlets.

Dad was very successful in his businesses and a very good provider for his family. His business ventures eventually meant a move for the family from my beloved homestead into town.

Preparing to Fulfill My Destiny

Say to the skillful and godly Wisdom, You are my sister, and
regard understanding or insight as your intimate friend.
Proverbs 7:4

Right from the beginning I was the only one at home during the day while my older siblings all went off to school. With so many siblings and so much activity surrounding school, by the time I was four years old I wanted what they had. So I would sit on the bottom step of the staircase trying to do the arithmetic in my siblings' old schoolbooks. Naturally I was incapable of doing the work and would get frustrated!

As a five-year-old, staying at home with Mom had lost much of its appeal; life on the outside looked much more promising. After a winter of my staged protests and pestering, Mom finally gave in and allowed me to go to school in the spring, a good six months earlier than planned.

And so it was that at the ripe old age of five I found myself heading out the door early each morning with my brothers. I proudly carried my Roger's Syrup tin turned lunch pail and climbed up into the buggy behind the horses for the two-and-a-half mile trip to school in Dixon.

The country schoolhouse was typical for that time and place—one room, one teacher, eight grades—and it served all the families in our farming community. When grade 8 was completed, grades 9 and 10 could be done through correspondence if desired, with the teacher available for help. After grade 10, your schooling was done. Very few farm children went on for higher education.

Like any country school, everybody knew everybody and families often gathered there for events, so when I started going as a five-year-old, the school itself wasn't unfamiliar to me. Besides, I was so excited to finally be going to school, to be learning, I'm not sure it would have mattered if I hadn't know anyone or seen the building before that first day.

The day came when there was work to be done on the farm. Farm work always took precedence over attending school, so the boys had to stay home. As I was not allowed to take the horse and buggy by myself, I prepared to walk the two and a half miles. There were no school buses or public transportation, and no self-respecting parent would have even entertained the thought of driving their children a mere two and a half miles anywhere, let alone school!

Swinging my lunch pail, I happily left the house and walked the first half mile on the road, but I soon discovered that walking on the railroad tracks would be much more fun. I could walk the tracks for almost two miles before having to leave them to cross over to get to the school. It was an enjoyable time, skipping from one tie to the next, all alone in the great big world!

It seemed like I'd only been on the tracks for a few minutes when I heard a familiar sound behind me. I jumped off and turned around to see a jigger coming down the rails. This was not unusual, as they would come by every day to inspect the rails, making sure none were lifting, but it was a thrill to get to watch one up close. I watched the small hand car come closer and was enthralled to watch the jiggerman standing on the flat deck, pumping the arm in the centre of it up and down to move the car. As it came alongside of me, the jiggerman stomped his foot on the metal post centred on the side between the two wheels, engaging the brake and stopping the car.

Taking in the lunch pail and my size, he guessed that I was on my way to the only school in the area and asked if I wanted a ride. Without hesitation, as everyone in those parts in those days was to be trusted, I nodded, and he helped me climb onto the deck. There was plenty of room for me to either sit or stand, and I chose to stand as he began to pump the arm up and down, up and down, giving us momentum and building up speed. This was most certainly the way to travel, I thought, excited to experience yet another adventure.

When we came closer to the place where I would need to get off, he stopped pumping and let the jigger slow down before standing on the brake, stopping, and letting me off. With a wave and a huge thank-you I skipped the last little way to school, eager to tell anyone who would listen how I got to school that morning.

Forever after I would walk the tracks when I was alone, hoping to time my journey to coincide with the jiggerman's, and whenever he came down the track and saw me, he would stop to give me a ride.

School was everything I expected. I excelled in my studies, doing the first four grades in only three years, but unfortunately I could not seem to pick up on spelling. We were taught to read by memorizing long columns of words, which we had to read off without a break. I knew that spelling would always plague me, and I also struggled to read out loud. It would embarrass me later on in the convent when I would have to take my turn reading out loud during meals. I don't know who suffered more from my reading, me or my listeners. It was only after I began teaching singers to sing in Italian years later that I learned to read out loud, as every vowel in Italian is spoken, meaning each one has to be really looked at.

One of the highlights of our one-room country school was Christmas, when we would perform a concert for our families. One year my mom made cream puffs for a program that my brothers were in. I was so dismayed to see them flying across the stage as part of the Christmas drama instead of being allowed to eat them! I can't remember any other concert in particular. I just loved the pageantry of it all, the excitement of performances, whether watching or being part of them. Drama and music pulled at my heart.

When I was in grade 5, my older brother Mike got married and took over the farm. By this time Dad already had his business running in Humboldt, selling machinery and fertilizer, so he made the decision to move the family into town.

Humboldt is 113 kilometres east of Saskatoon and became an official town in 1907. In 1944, when we moved there, it was by far the largest town in the area. There were smaller communities all around it but none that held the importance of Humboldt. There wasn't much missing from the town; it even had a theatre and a bowling alley!

There were two elementary schools in Humboldt, a public school and a private Roman Catholic one run by the Ursuline nuns. I attended the Catholic school, the Humboldt Separate School, in grade 5.

I was excited that first day. Sitting in my desk, I listened as the Sister asked who would like to take music lessons. My hand shot up immediately. You see, I had asked my parents if I could have piano lessons, but I was told that because no one else had had lessons in the family, it wouldn't be fair. Now I was being asked if I wanted to take music lessons. I wasn't going to turn that down!

I saw no reason to tell anyone at home about the lessons. I would be practicing at the music house, where the lessons were to take place, and I had figured out a way to pay for them myself. The lessons were one dollar a week. I earned twenty-five cents for my allowance each week, and I knew that four times a quarter equalled one dollar. In my ten-year-old mind, that meant I had enough money. I hadn't calculated the fact that there are four weeks in a month, not four quarters in a week!

By Christmas I realized that I couldn't continue. While it saddened me, it was just one of those things that happened in life, and I put it behind me. I had all but forgotten about it when in January I came home one afternoon to find my parents sitting at the kitchen table with a bill for music lessons in front of them. Fear welled up from deep inside me, and I just stared at them.

It felt like years before someone spoke. Dad finally looked up at me and asked me what this bill was about. It all spilled out of me, every detail, from the first day of school to thinking I could manage to pay for it myself and how I had miscalculated my income. His response was that I would have to stop, but because I had already done that, I didn't feel like I was being punished. Quite the opposite, actually. I felt like I'd been given a reprieve.

Going to the Humboldt Separate School was a big change from our little one-room schoolhouse. For one thing, there were now Sisters to teach us, and I was very much in awe of them and very afraid of making mistakes. I was also a farm girl and used to knowing everyone in my school back in Dixon. Now I was the outcast, not knowing a soul.

It took a while for me to make friends and get used to the new school. One day I was so frustrated at being the odd one out that I bit a girl! I'm not sure how I thought that would help matters, but at the time it seemed to be my only outlet for the negative feelings I had. I'm surprised that it only earned me a talking to, because not long after that I received the strap for making three spelling mistakes!

As children do, I adjusted, and I grew to love the Sisters and the school. I made good friends for the first time in my life and had a close bond with one Sister in particular, Sister Mary Herman. She was already special to our family, as I was named after her. My parents knew her family, and I even stayed at her mother's place when my mom and dad were out of town. Sister Mary Herman was a fantastic musician, gifted in both piano and voice. While I was in the separate school, she gave me voice lessons, even successfully entering me into a festival. I worshiped her and thought she could do no wrong. It couldn't get more holy, could it, but to be a nun and gifted with music? I practiced twice as hard for her, not wanting to ever disappoint her. Sister Mary Herman would be a constant in my life right through my school years and all through my own years as a nun.

The separate school only went to grade 8. There were two options for grade 9 and beyond, one being the local public high school, the other St. Ursula's Academy, a boarding school for girls. My parents were afraid that if I went to the public school I would be derailed from my future as a nun, so they sent me to St. Ursula's, even though it was not publicly funded and none of my sisters had gone there.

The boarding school, or academy, was located in Bruno, a community seventeen miles east of Humboldt, and was housed in the same building as the convent. The building itself, which would become my home for the next four years, had been built in 1919, when Bruno was chosen as the new location for the motherhouse for the nuns. The academy itself was founded in 1922.

Ursuline boarding schools began in France hundreds of years earlier when the Ursuline Sisters there adopted two significant elements to their order: papal enclosure (usually referred to as *cloister*) and solemn vows. Papal cloister forbade the nuns to leave the convent grounds except for serious reasons, and solemn vows (chastity, poverty, and obedience) signified that they were surrendering any claims to earthly things. Cloistered nuns could only visit with their families a few times a year and then only in the convent from behind a grill, a small window covered by wooden latticework. One or two nuns were allowed to do business in the town, but the other Sisters were not to go out of the cloister.

When these two elements were adopted, it put a sudden end to the mission work that the Sisters were carrying out outside of the convent, specifically teaching. So the Ursulines formed boarding schools, bringing girls to a separate section of the convent to live and be taught.

The nuns that came to Saskatchewan in 1913 were part of a community in Germany that traced their beginnings back to the Ursulines in France and still held the observances of a strict cloister and solemn vows. In St. Peter's Colony, the Sisters lived in small mission houses and taught school outside of the convent grounds, making strict cloister impossible to keep. They had to receive a dispensation from Rome in order to continue teaching. This meant that they were absolved from the rules of solemn vows and were allowed out of the cloister. Nonetheless, when they built the convent they did so intending to keep the purpose of the Ursuline nuns, the teaching of young girls.

It was 1949 when I entered St. Ursula's Academy to begin my high school years. I was excited, as I already knew some of the girls and the Sisters, but nervous because it was another huge change. I had never been in the school before, and it was a little intimidating to drive up to the huge three-storey brick building. It didn't take long to find my way around, however, as each floor served a distinct purpose.

The basement held the kitchen, laundry facilities, and dining room. On the first, or main, floor were the academy's classrooms to the right and the chapel off to the left. It wasn't a very impressive chapel, having only two stained glass windows at the front and no choir loft. It was a simple long room with the altar at the front and the organ at the back.

The girls would sit in the front pews, and the Sisters would sit behind them.

The second floor was set aside as the convent and completely off limits to us students. It wasn't until the new addition was built and this floor was used as part of the academy that any of us saw where the Sisters did their living and schooling. Our sleeping quarters were in the dorms on the third floor, where each girl had her own curtained-off area.

As I was adjusting to the new surroundings and getting used to living away from home, I was pleased to find out that a group of six or eight of us girls, from all grades, would form a family with a Sister assigned to us as a convent mother. I was even more pleased to find out that my hero, Mother Mary Herman, would be my convent mother. Like a mother she would make sure we were well-mannered and that our clothing was kept in good repair, checking that we kept up with our studies and even checking our incoming and outgoing mail. Mother Mary Herman would be my convent mother for the entire four years I was a student there.

The discipline was quite strict in the academy and the days regimented. Monday to Saturday, all the girls wore navy blue jumpers that came three inches below our knees, with tan blouses underneath. On Sunday we wore navy dresses with small white collars. Silence in the dorms was strictly enforced, and homework had to be done. If everything was in order, we would be allowed to take books out of the library. I loved to read, and over the course of my four years, I may have read half the books in the library.

Every afternoon in recreation time we played games or went for walks if the weather permitted, and Saturday afternoons were usually free time. This was when we dedicated ourselves to fun, although sometimes our fun cost us some of our free time.

It was a cold and snowy Saturday, much like all the other winter days in Saskatchewan, but we didn't let that stop us from having our afternoon fun. After all our chores were done and lunch was behind us, my friends and I put on our winter jackets, boots, mittens, and hats and went outside, grabbing our toboggans. We laughed and ran down the road for several miles to get to the one hill that could be tobogganed

27

down. It wasn't very big, but we were thankful just to have a hill. We had a great time climbing up and then flying down, but after an hour or so we knew we had to start heading back.

As we were walking back to the school, a car came down the road behind us. It slowed as it came near, and we waved our arms at them to stop. We boldly asked if we could tie our toboggans to the bumper of their car and get a ride back to Bruno. This wasn't the first time we had done that, and we had yet to be turned down. The driver agreed, and we quickly tied our toboggans on, hopped on, and held on. This was as exhilarating to me as those rides with the jiggerman back in my early elementary school days.

As we approached the edge of town, the driver slowed and stopped to let us off. We had asked to be dropped off there, hoping to be far enough from the academy that the Sisters would not see us. Riding behind cars on toboggans was strictly against the rules. Usually this worked, but not this particular day. We were found out and were given a severe talking to, which included the loss of a few Saturday privileges. As I recall there were a few such punishments over the years for the wrong choice of travel.

The main purpose of the Ursuline nuns was to teach us, and their academic standards were very high. Yet, even with having to meet those standards, I enjoyed school and found classes interesting, especially history and literature. The Sisters had a vast amount of knowledge and made classes very thought-provoking.

Academics, however, were secondary to our spiritual training, which was woven throughout our day and into our studies. From mealtimes to quiet times to the reading material available, everything was under the authority of God, and we were expected to behave accordingly.

Every morning we headed into the chapel for Mass and every evening for night prayers. Religious studies were part of our curriculum, and every student was expected to spend time in meditation and prayer. To enhance our spiritual growth, the academy held a retreat every spring where a retreat master, a priest, would come in to speak to us three times a day. For three days we were to focus intensely on our spiritual lives, with the purpose of growing our faith. There were times of meditation, worship, solitude, and prayer, and all of our reading material was on the lives of saints.

Barely seven months into my first year of boarding school, still in grade 9 and only fourteen years old, I experienced my first retreat, which immersed me in the Catholic faith. I devoured all manner of holy books, reading about the lives of the saints, observing the silence, and listening to the sermons. This intense spiritual time led me to believe that this was what the religious life was all about, sure that the retreat was a glimpse into what life would be like as a nun. Everything that I experienced during that retreat confirmed what I was raised to be. There was no stretching of my imagination needed to see myself in a life of full-time spiritual retreat, and I was never more convinced of my future.

When two girls in grade 12 approached the Mother Superior about entering the convent in the fall and were encouraged to follow that path, I felt compelled to do the same. In the midst of what felt totally holy and inspiring to me, and knowing that my future was in this convent, I too asked the Mother Superior if I could enter the convent.

Very gently she encouraged me to wait until I had completed high school. Having no choice but to be obedient to her wishes, that is what I did.

And so I continued with classes and my music lessons. Music programs and cultivating a love of music were a large part of the Ursuline culture, and many students came to the academy because of its musical reputation. Since the 1930s the Sisters had been running the Humboldt Ursuline Music Studio in a six-room house, beginning with piano lessons. When Sister Mary Herman joined the convent she brought with her an associate diploma in voice from the Toronto Conservatory of Music as well as a licentiate diploma from Trinity College in London. Voice lessons were then also offered at the studio, and each year the Sisters organized the annual Humboldt Music Festival.

Having already taken a few voice lessons from Sister Mary Herman and a few piano lessons in elementary school and having felt the tug of the stage on the balcony of our farmhouse years earlier, it didn't take long for me to completely and eagerly immerse myself in both piano and voice. In my four years of high school I completed my Royal Conservatory grade 10 piano as well as my grade 5 voice, both the highest level of achievement possible before getting performance degrees.

With my passion for music and the stage, it was natural for me to join the academy's glee club, directed by Mother Mary Herman (having been in the convent for ten years by then she was no longer a Sister but a Mother). It had a reputation all over the province for a high quality of music, and I couldn't wait to be part of it. We didn't travel much, but each year we entered the Humboldt Festival and we sang a Christmas cantata. Every girl in the glee club would hold her breath, hoping to get a choice solo part in the performance.

My passions also drew me to drama class. We would act out skits all year long, and once a year we would stage a full-length play in the basement of the parish church. I found myself drawn to the costuming as much as the music and drama. One of my favourite things to do in my spare time was to pore over the Simpsons-Sears' and Eaton's catalogues and study the dress designs, then turning to the fabric section to pick out fabric. For the skits and plays, I would go through the exquisite materials that had been brought over from Germany, looking to create the needed costumes. Considering that we were not allowed to cut any of the fabric, it was quite a challenge, but I loved it.

By the time I entered my last year of high school, the desire and eagerness that I had felt in grade 9 to enter the convent had moved over to allow a place for my discovery of music and the stage. Not only did I have a passion for it all, I had the talent to go along with it, and when I entered grade 12 I decided I might pursue a singing career at the Toronto Conservatory of Music after high school. I had spoken to Dad about it, but all he said was "Well, if you do, don't come back and marry some farmer." It was one of the few times Dad really spoke to me. While it wasn't exactly helpful or encouraging, he also didn't forbid me, so I changed some of my courses to fit the requirements for university.

During my final year as a student at the academy, the glee club entered the music festival in Saskatoon for the first time. I had several solos that I was to perform in the festival and was quite nervous.

The time finally arrived. We were all nervous, as this was a new experience. To make matters worse, the day we were to sing our accompanist broke out in measles! With a lot of makeup she was still able to play for us that day, but the next day she was too sick to accompany me on my solos. With no other choice, Mother Mary Herman filled in the gap. We were shocked that she would do this, because the Sisters were not allowed to be seen in public.

In one particular class of music I listened as several of the girls who went before me sang the same song I had prepared, with one exception: they sang it in French. When it was my turn I was so nervous that I started to sing in French! The problem was that I hadn't learned it in French, and I was horrified. I quickly changed back to English, and even with that rocky beginning I won a twenty-five dollar scholarship.

During my grade 12 year we were all thrilled to have the Von Trapp family come to our academy and perform. They even stayed with us, and it was exciting to have celebrities of sorts with us.

Soon it was time for our annual spring retreat; this would be the last one for me in high school. I had been taking all the courses I needed to go to university, but I was struggling with my choice because it would mean not becoming a nun. I decided to have a talk with Mother Mary Herman and get her perspective and advice.

I poured out my conflicting passions: music and the church. She pointed out that often when I sang in public I would over-sing and my voice would break. She sincerely believed it was a sign from the Lord that he didn't want me to go to Toronto. I didn't know at the time that it was just a lack of technique, so I took her words to heart and considered them greatly.

I kept wondering what I should do. With Mother Mary Herman's words echoing in my head, I couldn't shake the feeling that if I didn't enter the convent I would go to hell. It wasn't put into so many words, but I felt like following music would be my spiritual demise. At the age of seventeen, it was difficult for me to turn away from everything I had worked towards and that was expected of me, and it would greatly disappoint my family. When it came right down to it, the choice was an obvious one, even if not a comfortable one. And so I once again asked the Mother Superior if I could enter the convent, and I was accepted.

Our grade 12 graduation ceremonies were held on the same day that Queen Elizabeth II was crowned. It fell on a weekday, so very few of my family could attend. I wore a white dress that passed inspection, as it was long-sleeved, high necked, and deemed modest enough. I would wear the same dress as a bride of Christ when I entered my second year as a nun.

That summer, my last before entering the convent, I attended the Banff School of Fine Arts, as it had been decided that I was to be a music teacher. Mother Mary Herman came along as my chaperone, and we walked to school together and took all the classes together. I was given accommodation in the nurses' residence at the hospital rather than in the dorms with the students, and Mother Mary Herman stayed with the Sisters in the hospital.

I met a very nice girl who was a practical nurse, and I was given some free time to go to movies or to town with her. One evening we met two Greek men who had come to Canada very recently. One of them took a real shine to me, and I couldn't get rid of him. While it was a new experience having a man interested in me and I was flattered, I really had no interest in him. I found it quite amusing that he would wait for me in places, phone me, and tell me he wanted to marry me. If only Mother Mary Herman knew the trouble I was getting into!

I thoroughly enjoyed my classes that summer. I sat in on piano master classes, where I learned how to memorize a piece of music away from the piano. I also took a vocal class where we performed the opera *Martha*. All these classes would serve me well in the convent, as I planned to continue to study music and eventually teach, but it also gave me a feel for the career that a part of me still longed for.

Yet as the day grew closer for me to enter the convent, my focus grew more and more towards the Lord, and I made complete peace with my decision. Once I had committed myself, my love affair with Jesus took hold, and I couldn't wait to serve him full time and to devote the rest of my life to him.

Becoming a Bride of Christ

My beloved speaks and says to me,
Rise up, my love, my fair one, and come away.
Song of Solomon 2:10

It was 6 a.m. on Saturday, September 5, 1953. I woke up to the sound of a bell, which told me I was no longer in my bed at the farm on a harvesting day. It only took a moment for me to take in my surroundings and remember this was my first day as a nun.

I was a nun! I felt the excitement of the previous day take hold again. As I faced my first full day as a postulant, I felt excited to begin a life that would be one endless spring retreat. Just me and Jesus in constant communication.

Lying there those first few minutes in the quiet of the day, I knew I had forty-five minutes before the next bell rang. I shared my new room with six novices and my fellow postulant, Delores. At this time of day each Sister had the curtain pulled around her own space, creating what was called a cell. Each one looked identical to mine, with a white metal-framed cot taking up the majority of the small space. On my right sat a straight-backed wooden chair, and facing it beside the foot of the bed was a wooden washstand. The bottom of the stand was a cupboard where I kept my personal things, such as underwear, stockings, and such. A pitcher and basin sat on the stand, used for my sponge baths. There was a serious water shortage at the time, and until a proper well was dug we rarely had a real bath. I had two towels, one to be used for my upper body, the other for the lower half.

While the setup of the room was much the same as our dorm rooms in the academy, our quarters were in the new motherhouse, an addition to the old building, and it was still being completed. The old convent on the second floor of the brick building was now used for the academy, which had been growing. The new house held two parlours, a chapel, a dining hall, a kitchen, and a novitiate, where the postulants and novices lived and learned.

I pulled myself out of the luxury of my bed and began what I knew to be my expected daily routine. I made my bed, had my sponge bath, dressed, and tidied up my washstand, covering the stand with a cloth so it wouldn't be visible to others. I then opened the curtains and tied them to the left of my bed. I checked and rechecked my cell, knowing that cleanliness was important and that a check by the senior Sisters could happen at any time of the day.

As expected, the next bell rang at 6:45 a.m. This one indicated that Office was about to begin and we were expected in the chapel. As we were still in the time of the Great Silence, there was no speaking as we moved out of our room and downstairs to the chapel.

Silence was nothing new to me, as our spring retreats were done mostly in silence, and the students at the academy respected the Sisters' silence, but the Great Silence was a little quieter than I was used to. Nonetheless, I embraced it wholeheartedly in my eagerness.

I followed the other Sisters to the chapel. Our entrance led to the wing where only the nuns sat, out of view of the main body of the church where the academy girls sat.

This new chapel was designed as an inverted L, with the short end being the nuns' area and the long section the main part. Along the side of the main body were windows that, as finances and time allowed, were made into beautiful stained glass windows. Using symbols designed by one of our nuns, artist Andre Rault of France created the windows, which depicted significant mysteries of the faith. It would take ten years for all eight windows to be completed.

Each window was as magnificent as the last, made with heavy glass pieces bonded by lead. When the sun shone through them, it was truly awe-inspiring and would cause any gloomy mood to lift instantly. Gazing on those windows, with or without sunlight streaming through them, we could contemplate the mysteries that they represented: I Am the Life; Wisdom and Understanding; Sing to the Lord; Send Forth Thy Spirit; I Am the Mother of Fair Love; I Am the Vine; Glory Be to the Trinity; and Christ, The Physician.

At the front of the chapel were two alcoves, one on each side of the altar. The Blessed Virgin rested in the alcove on the left, a statue of Jesus on the right. Between the alcoves and against the wall was a simple altar, two marble pillars holding up a marble slab. Covering it was a hand-embroidered altar cloth.

Above the main entrance was the choir loft, which also housed the organ. If we were singing a special number or there was a visiting choir, this was where the music came from. The music would soar over and around those beneath the loft. When I heard the voices surround me I imagined that it was the sound I would one day hear in heaven.

On this first morning as a nun I realized that I would have to do some serious learning in order to know not only the routine of the convent but also the proper protocol that was observed. The first thing I learned was that everything was done in silence. Different from the Great Silence, when to speak was to be punished, the general silence was just the norm as we went about our day. We spoke only when absolutely necessary and during our recreation times, that half hour after our noon meal and hour after our evening meal. Our entire being was centred on the spiritual, and therefore idle chit-chat was not part of our day.

As a postulant and for the two years as a novice, I ate my meals at a separate table with other postulants and novices and shared recreation time with them as well. There was a distinct separation between those who had taken vows and those who had not.

This was my first morning as a nun in the chapel, and, just as we had the afternoon and evening before, we gathered to say the Office. The word *Office* comes from the Latin word *Officium,* meaning "duty," and the purpose of it is to give praise and glory to God throughout all hours of the day. Office itself is made up of the 150 psalms of the Old Testament and is divided throughout the seven days of the week. In addition to the psalms there are sacred readings, prayers, and short accounts of the lives of the saints. Office is divided into eight hours, which are not sixty-minute time periods but rather represent the eight parts that complete a day and a cycle of hours. For example, *matins* and *lauds* are the first two hours, representing midnight and the time before dawn. *Prime* is the hour of dawn, and *terce* is the hour for midmorning. The midday hour is *sext*, midafternoon is *none*, *vespers* is dusk, and the day is finished with *compline*, representing the time after sunset. Saying the eight hours of Office each day ensured that we were giving God all the glory and praise due him throughout every hour of the day.

Saying the Office, while beautiful, was difficult for me at first and didn't get easier until I learned the Latin that they were written in. Until then I was quite grateful for the English translation on the opposite page in the prayer book. At least I knew what was being said and could follow along in my heart.

After we said our Office that first morning there was half an hour of meditation. It was a pleasure that morning to just sit and contemplate Scripture. I had so much to think about, so much to meditate on. It was all new, and I was so eager to learn and to please.

After our time of meditation the students from the academy arrived, along with the parish priest, and together we observed Mass. At the end of Mass the Great Silence was broken, but as we all headed to the dining room it was still silent. The only difference was that if we felt compelled to speak now it was not going to cost us penance.

Breakfast was a very simple affair; porridge and bread and butter was the daily fare, along with coffee for those who wanted it. Six days a week it was the same, but on Sunday we had a special breakfast, cold cereal and toast. It doesn't sound like much to me now, but it was a real treat then after the daily porridge.

I was a little surprised after breakfast when we were assigned household chores to do. I expected that we might have to help with clearing and doing the dishes, but I presumed that then I would be immersed in reading of the saints or doing everything spiritual, not cleaning bathrooms, mopping floors, cleaning our classrooms, or dusting and polishing. Still, these were our only chores, as there were lay Sisters who did the more menial work. Lay Sisters were women who did not have much education and did the cooking, laundry, farming, and the growing of food and flowers. They could not take part in the governing of our community, and their prayers were different from ours. They also did not say Office, because they had not studied Latin. I used to feel sorry for them, as they did such hard physical work, but their examples of humility and hard work left quite an impression on me.

While we went about our daily chores, whether the menial work to keep things tidy or later the work that we were called to do, we were to keep our focus on God. In order to do that, every hour, on the hour, we stopped what we were doing to pray, "O Lord God, I give to thee this day, all I think or do or say, uniting it with what was done, on earth by Jesus Christ, thy Son." What a beautiful reminder to continually to give God everything I thought, did, or said!

After our housework we put our energies into our studies. The postulants and novices studied church history, rules of the order, and some Scriptures. In addition I studied Latin and music, working on my piano and voice. Midmorning we were allowed to take a break and go down to the dining room for a cup of coffee or tea, and it was nice to stretch and move around. We always had our break standing up, and of course it was all in silence.

There were times that first day where I almost broke the silence. It took a little bit of getting used to for me to be so quiet. My passions were drama and the stage, and it was just natural for me to talk.

After lunch it was back to the chapel as individuals to take five minutes to examine ourselves. There I was, a nun for barely one day, and I was already looking at myself to see what I might have done wrong that morning. It was expected that errors had been made, and I knew there were many things that I would need to work on.

Once that examination was done we had thirty minutes of recreation. The silence was lifted, and we were free to do needlework or crafts or even take a walk if the weather was nice. I was still working on putting the number eighty-three on all my belongings and reminding myself to have a proper nun-like attitude about it.

More studying followed, broken up at 3:30 and 5:30 for more Offices. After the last one we had thirty minutes of meditation again before dinner. Dinner was also a simple meal, with much of our food grown in our own garden. I helped clean up afterwards, and then it was back to the needlework and number eighty-three!

The day ended like the one previous with night prayers. Following the formal prayers several Sisters lay face down on the floor of the chapel with their arms stretched out wide. I soon learned that this was a way of finishing our personal prayers, an act of submission, being prostrate before the Lord. It was left entirely up to each Sister whether or not she wished to do it.

And so my first complete day as a nun ended. There was so much to take in that I was pretty tired, trying hard to remember everything that I needed to for the next day.

Each day following was a little easier than the one previous, and the biggest relief for me that first week was when I finally did my last stitch on my belongings, making them officially belonging to me, number eighty-three.

As a postulant I had been given five balls of black yarn. From this I was to make a "girdle," which I would wear over my habit like a belt when I became a novice. Using six or eight strands I wove the yarn together into a long round rope. It was then sewn together to go around my waist three times. When I completed this I kept it in my locker in anticipation of the spring, when I would begin the next phase of being a nun, entering the novitiate.

Life as a nun wasn't all that hard once I became accustomed to what was expected of me and learned more Latin. In some ways I was on probation, as that first year I was making sure that my calling was real and was being watched very closely by the Sisters for the same reason. You would think that would make me very careful about everything I did, and for the most part I was, but I was still an eighteen-year-old farm girl at heart.

Although a life of poverty, chastity and obedience was what I had chosen, occasionally I would forget myself. One wintery day, the kind that just called out for fun, Delores and I were on a walk when we found some huge snowbanks. We had a great time building tunnels in those snowbanks and crawling through them. Unfortunately, we were in the nuns' cemetery at the time. Our digging, even though it was all just in snow, was considered "desecrating" the graves, and so we were properly chastised. By the time spring came around, the incident was forgotten, or not deemed serious, and I was still allowed to pursue becoming a nun.

As I finished off my first year in the convent, I was surprised to realize that I hadn't entered into the relationship with Jesus that I had dreamed about. While a good deal of my day was spent in holy activities and meditations, the day-to-day activities seemed to take the joy out of my dream. I couldn't seem to get to the place where Jesus would meet me and everything would be glorious. So much of my energies were still in learning, though, so I anticipated that as I delved further and further into being a committed servant of Christ, the relationship would develop. To that end I was fully committed and ready to become a novice.

I would be giving up my postulant clothing and receiving an actual habit; I would be giving up my name and receiving a new one; and the days and the routine would be much stricter. In my mind this was all just one step closer to that relationship I dreamed about and longed for.

The day for Delores and me to become novices finally arrived in May. Our families were invited to the chapel to witness the ceremony. That morning I did not put on the dress that I had worn for the past eight months. Instead I took out the white dress that I wore for my high school graduation at the academy. Wearing white, I was dressed as a bride, and I was coming to Jesus as his bride on this day.

Delores and I entered the chapel and made our way forward to where the abbot was waiting. The abbot was the spiritual leader of St. Peter's Colony and the spiritual overseer of the convent, the go-between between us and Rome. We approached him and asked to be admitted to the novitiate.

We were accepted, and as a symbol of dying to our old selves we lay face down on the floor. The Sisters covered us with a black cloth as prayers were said over us. When the cloth was removed we stood up and prepared to enter a new life. We were given our new clothing and head gear, and with that in hand we left the chapel to get changed.

Our new garments were completely plain from the inside out. All but the stockings were made by the lay Sisters, including the cotton bras and underwear. The hose that we received that day were not the heavy black wool ones, as we were coming up to summer, but instead were a lighter material, although still black.

I put on the ill-fitting undergarments and then the hose. On top of this I pulled on a black slip, over which I tied a string around my waist that held my pocket, where I would keep my personal rosary and extra hankies, having access to it through two slits in my habit. Over all this went my habit, which was made very simply from black serge. Pleats fell from the large yokes in the front and in the back, and the sleeves that came off the yoke were very wide and long. In order to never show any skin, I wore a pair of black sleeves that fit snugly from my elbow to my wrist. I would learn to stand with my hands inside my wide sleeves at all times.

To cinch the habit to my body I brought out the girdle that I had made from yarn, and, because as a novice I hadn't yet taken my vows, I wrapped it three times around my waist. On my head I wore what was known as a gimp, a highly starched bib that completely encircled my face. My forehead was covered with a white band, and over all of it I wore a huella, a starched white cloth that held the white veil. Heavy black oxford shoes completed my outfit.

The last thing to be added to my habit was the external rosary, which was suspended from my girdle. This was purely as a reminder to pray the rosary once a day.

Once we were dressed and in perfect order we entered the chapel again. I was given the name Sister Mary Michael, the Kingship of Christ, and Delores became Sister Tarcisia. The new names were a symbol of a new life, representing the old life passing away. I had requested the name of Michael but was not expecting to receive it, as many other Sisters had requested it and been refused, and a name is never used twice. Michael is spoken of in the Bible in one of Daniel's visions as a chief prince battling with the king of Persia (commonly thought of as one of Satan's demons) for the Israelites. I was thrilled to receive that name, and the irony of having a warrior's name when my own father fled to get out of the army was not lost on me.

After the ceremony we were allowed to visit with our families and even have pictures taken. I hoped I made my mother proud that day as she watched that second ceremony in the chapel, seeing me in my habit. It was wonderful to see her again and have a visit.

The next morning I woke up and put on the clothing that I would wear every day for the rest of my life. It took a little more time to get dressed than before because of the different layers and making sure everything was in perfect order.

As usual I attached my rosary last. The rosary of course had always been part of my life. As a child and even more so later on as a young adult I would hear my parents say the rosary together, which was such a reassuring and comforting thing.

As I handled the long string of beads and arranged it so that it looped just so with the large cross hanging down in the front, I thought about its significance and history, how it is used for God's people to make the day holy and to remember the life of Jesus and his mother. It is a collection of prayers that keep the devout faithful.

There are different schools of thought as to where the first rosary originated, but praying on beads began as a parallel to the psalms. As far back as the ninth century the religious orders recited all 150 psalms together daily. This was done in Latin, and when people heard the beautiful sound they wanted to follow their example. There were a few problems with trying to put this in practice. It was too lengthy to memorize, especially in Latin, and even if there were copies in print for them to memorize, most of the people were illiterate.

It was decided that they would say 150 "Our Fathers" throughout the day, which is the Lord's prayer taken from Matthew 6:9-13. This was their way of having the spiritual connection that the monks did. At first they kept count of their prayers with pebbles in a pouch, but in later years they counted on a string knotted with 150 knots. Eventually that turned into the rosary with beads we have today.

There is also a common belief that Mary herself appeared to St. Dominic early in the 13th century and gave him the rosary as a weapon to be used against the heresy sweeping Europe at the time, and he made the rosary his devotion.

Whatever the accurate history, the rosary was a significant part of my life. My rosary, the same since the Middle Ages, contained fifty beads, divided into five decades of ten beads with a big bead separating the decades. There are three mysteries that we focus on at different times of the year, and within each mystery there are five parts.

In my year as a postulant I had learned that if I got up as soon as the morning bell rang and worked quickly to ready myself and my cell I would have time to say the rosary before breakfast and have one of my spiritual disciplines done for the day. It wasn't an easy task; nor could I cut corners in saying it. I could, however, say it pretty fast.

That first morning as a novice I was all dressed and ready for my next part of the journey as a nun. Even though it had taken a little longer to get dressed, I still had time for my rosary. I reached my hands through the slits in my habit, took my small rosary out of my pocket, and sat on my chair. With my eyes closed and holding the cross at the beginning of my rosary, I made the sign of the cross and recited the Apostles' Creed.

"I believe in God the Father Almighty, Maker of heaven and earth. And in Jesus Christ his only Son our Lord; who was conceived by the Holy Ghost, born of the Virgin Mary, suffered under Pontius Pilate, was crucified, dead, and buried; he descended into hell. The third day he rose again from the dead; he ascended into heaven, and sitteth on the right hand of God the Father Almighty. From thence he shall come to judge the quick and the dead. I believe in the Holy Ghost; the holy catholic church; the communion of saints; the forgiveness of sins; the resurrection of the body; and the life everlasting. Amen."

I moved my hand automatically to the bead next to the cross and reverently recited an Our Father.

"Our Father, who art in heaven, hallowed be thy name; thy kingdom come; thy will be done on earth as it is in heaven. Give us this day our daily bread; and forgive us our trespasses as we forgive those who trespass against us; and lead us not into temptation, but deliver us from evil. Amen."

I immediately moved my fingers to the next three beads and recited three Hail Marys. "Hail Mary, full of grace. The Lord is with thee. Blessed art thou amongst women, and blessed is the fruit of thy womb, Jesus. Holy Mary, Mother of God, pray for us sinners, now and at the hour of our death. Amen."

By feel and by rote I found the next bead, larger than the previous three, which told me to say the Glory Be to the Father. "Glory be to the Father, and to the Son, and to the Holy Spirit, as it was in the beginning, is now, and ever shall be, world without end. Amen."

From there I moved into the body of the rosary. First I announced the mystery that I would be contemplating as I said the rest of my rosary. Because it was May and after Easter, the Sorrowful Mystery was behind us, where we had contemplated Christ's agony in the garden, his scourging at the pillar, being crowned with thorns, the carrying of his cross, and his crucifixion.

I announced The Glorious Mystery and recited the Our Father.

The next bead was large and required me to say the first part of the mystery, that being the resurrection of Christ. Then followed ten small beads and ten Hail Marys. From there the rosary continued in the same way, with a large bead announcing another subsection of the mystery, followed by ten small beads that heralded Hail Marys. The other four parts of the mystery were the ascension, the descent of the Holy Spirit, the assumption and the coronation.

The other mystery that coincided with the time on the church calendar before Christmas was the Joyful Mystery, which encompassed the annunciation of Christ's birth, the visitation, the nativity, and the presentation of Jesus and the finding of him in the temple.

Saying the rosary took some time, but I found it to be a very good way to start my day, with a focus on prayer, meditation, and the lives of Christ and Mary.

Life as a novice was much stricter than it was as a postulant. In addition to the housework expected daily, the novices often had to set the tables before meals. A half hour beforehand we were to go and help dish up the food for the girls in the academy and the nuns. We also had to do the refectory dishes and help with the washing of pots.

As novices, we now took part in Chapter. Chapter was always held on Thursdays after the 5:30 p.m. Office instead of personal meditation, and was the weekly time of confession. We all went to the community room and sat on long benches set against the walls. Mother Superior stood at the front of the room and led Chapter. At times she would give direction for everyone or admonition for the Sisters. Then we would approach her two by two and confess our sins committed during the previous week. This could have been anything from wasting thread or breaking the Great Silence to talking unnecessarily. We were only allowed a maximum of three sins each week, so if there were more we kept them until the next Chapter.

Once we had confessed our sins, we would duly receive our penance. Penance could be a certain number of Hail Marys, Our Fathers, or prayers, or we might be instructed to prostrate ourselves before the altar in the chapel.

Being a novice is a two-year process, at the end of which I would become a junior. It is taken much more seriously than the year of being a postulant. My studying of music was severely curtailed in my first year as novice, as the religious life was most important now. As well as continuing in my Latin courses, I studied the history of the Church and of the Ursuline order and wrote out the translations for the Office that was said on special feast days.

My days were filled with religion and my religious duties, which I fulfilled eagerly. Yet no matter how much work I put into my studies, I still seemed to be missing what I had been hoping for. Where was my love? Where was my soul connection to Jesus?

These questions came to me most often as I sat during meditation. I had expected this to be an extremely personal time with Christ, a time for me to focus on God's Word. I tried to get close to him during this time, but none of the meditation methods seemed to work for me. Instead I would read the psalms, the Gospels, and some of the Old Testament books that were stories. Still my mind would drift as I found myself longing for the presence of Jesus and then, as often as not, falling asleep. I often had to do penance on Thursdays for falling asleep during meditation, and more than once the jab of a sister's elbow woke me up to focus back on my meditation. Each day I vowed to try harder, to give more.

The most enjoyable times to me were the hours and half hours of recreation. As well as learning how to do needlework, making tablecloths and altar cloths, we started writing plays to be put on for the community. We created spoofs on various aspects of life in the convent as well as dramatizing stories such as Winnie the Pooh. We had been schooled in drama in the academy, and it was carried on as we became nuns. It helped us all to combat the strictness of the convent, and the laughter was great medicine.

Something always came alive in me when we were practicing and preparing for a drama. There was a spark that was fanned with every performance. I never discussed this with any of the others, so I never knew whether this was a normal reaction or if there was something different in me.

When harvest time came around we helped in the fields. It was a joy to go pick up potatoes, because silence was dispensed with. We had the rare opportunity to have more time to chat with each other. We also helped shell peas and corn and prepared foods for canning. It took a lot of food to feed ninety girls and fifty nuns!

Feast days were times of joy for us all. There were small feast days celebrating name days, associated with the names that were given to us as novices. For example, when I became Sister Michael, September 29 became my name day, my own feast day. Other feast days were much more important, such as Christmas, Easter, St. Angela's Day (she began the company of St. Ursula in Italy in 1535), and in the summer Mother Superior Day. On the major celebrations there were special meals and food. I loved to help in the kitchen on those occasions, making bread, cakes, and other treats.

September 29 had arrived, my very first name day. At breakfast there was a small bouquet of flowers adorning my place, and each Sister offered me her greeting, albeit silently. At the end of the day I found my bed covered with little flowers and holy cards from the Sisters, offering congratulations and prayers for the occasion. Being singled out as special one day of the year was a big deal and one I treasured.

Before I knew it my first year as novice ended and I was in my second year. This would be my last before becoming a junior, which would mean taking my first vows. During this second year in the novitiate I began preparing for the work that I would be doing in the community, which was teaching music. That involved more and more practicing in order to get my degrees in both piano and voice. This was pure pleasure for me as I loved music.

One aspect of studying music that drew me was composing, and I wrote some songs for special feast days, as the liturgy was changing from Latin to English. I loved composing, but aside from that specific purpose it was discouraged and thought of as a waste of time.

I studied long and hard as I prepared to take my first vows. As I began to contemplate the vows of chastity, obedience, and poverty, I still could not rid myself completely of some worldly things. Simple things, like curtains on windows. There were no curtains on the windows of our novitiate, and I often longed for the comforting presence of such homey things. My mother had always made our homes beautiful, and the whole idea of decorating a home was a bit of a dream for me. It was closely tied to the drama that I loved and the costuming I was always involved in. The fabrics were so beautiful, the textures so varied and rich, I could imagine what it would be like to be able to have my own home with all the pretty things.

I really had a difficult time balancing these desires with the vows of poverty that I would be taking, and I began to question my vocation, the call to religious life. And because I had yet to discover Jesus, I was beginning to feel discouraged.

As I was nearing the end of my second year as a novice, my third year in the convent, I spoke to the novice mistress about my confusion and the longings that didn't seem to diminish as time went on. She told me not to worry about it; those feelings would go away.

I truly wanted to believe her and to serve the Lord, and I prepared to take my first vows.

Taking My Vows

For You, O God, have heard my vows; You have given me the
heritage of those who fear, revere, and honor Your name.
Psalm 61:5

Once again I walked up the aisle of the chapel, knowing that by moving forward I was making yet another change in my life. This was the third time I was making a memorable walk. The first time I entered, three years previously, I was still a naive school girl with a passion for Jesus and a desire to devote the rest of my life to him. The second time I was just as passionate, ready to die to my old life and begin the serious work of becoming a nun, eagerly receiving my habit for my new life.

This third time I was no longer a school girl with a passion. Nor was I as thrilled about dying to my old self or as eager to take my first vows. My heart was confused, still wanting to serve Jesus as I knew him but also feeling the pull to music, the stage, and the world in general. I was within a year of having my degrees in both voice and piano, and the more I studied, the more passionate I became. I wondered how I could feel both called to be a nun and so drawn to the world. Taking my vows would be the next step to completely denying the world and all its pleasures, much more serious than just receiving the habit and veil of a novice. They weren't solemn vows made for life, but they were still vows, promises that I couldn't take lightly.

Dying to my old life, denying the world and its pleasures, was a struggle. The old life and the world for me was represented by music, which I loved almost as much as I loved Jesus. By now I was also very aware of the daily life of a nun, the rules that had to be followed, and the expectations I had to meet. I was beginning to see a religion that was dominated by regulations and rituals.

Being as devoted to the Lord as a nun had to be called for the ultimate sacrifice. I knew that was why it was a process to get to the stage of taking those first vows. It was something to be taken with the utmost seriousness. For the previous three years I had spent much time in prayer and quietness, preparing myself for it.

Even with all this confusion in me, the strongest pull was still to serve the Lord, so I trusted in the wisdom of the novice mistress and made the decision to take my vows. I was determined to make this religious vocation work, so I confidently walked to the front of the chapel where the abbot waited. I felt strongly that the Lord would be pleased with me and meet me at the next level. If I worked harder, had a better and holier attitude, I was sure the relationship was achievable.

My parents were sitting somewhere amongst those gathered for this ceremony, and I was aware that I was fulfilling my family's expectation of me. I felt proud to hold the honour of being a nun. It meant that, besides my own personal spiritual quest, I could pray my family into heaven while I worked hard for my own entry. I was ready.

I stood before the abbot and listened intently as he asked me if I was willing to accept the temporary vows of poverty, obedience, and chastity and to hold to them for the next three years. I responded with all my heart that yes, I accepted them, knowing that I was turning my back to the world's pleasure—at least for the next three years.

I was still wearing the white veil of a novice. After I had taken the vows, the Sisters came forward and slipped a black veil over my white one, attached it to the huella, and then removed my white veil from underneath.

The only other change to my habit was the girdle. Before my vows it was tied three times around my waist. Now that I was a junior, it was loosened and only tied around my waist twice. The extra length that hung down the side of my habit was knotted into three knots to represent each vow that I took. Each time I tied my girdle around me I would feel the knots and be reminded of the promises of poverty, chastity, and obedience I had made on this day.

For the next three years before taking my solemn vows I would be a junior. As a junior, there were some major changes in my life. The first was that I moved out of the novitiate and into the body of the community. My new sleeping quarters were in a smaller room, which I now shared with only two other nuns. Recreation now included the other Sisters who had taken vows, and I also left the table in the dining room that was for postulants and novices and joined the Sisters at their table.

Once at this stage, we began to be more intentional about following our given careers within the convent. Those who were to be teachers went to university. I began teaching piano and voice under the supervision of Mother Angela. She was herself a very good piano teacher, and she would drop in on my lessons and check if my students were learning what they should.

When I entered the convent, I had already finished my grade 10 in piano and grade 5 in voice (then the equivalent of grade 10; it changed to ten levels a few years later). It was during my first year in the convent that I began working towards getting my associate degrees. As a junior those studies became even more important. Every two weeks four of us would drive to Saskatoon for lessons, and I was expected to have both of my degrees at the end of that year.

In order to foster good musicianship, the order engaged special clinicians to come to St. Ursula's to listen and critique us. One of these was Miss Dorothy Bee, who would come from Regina several times over the course of my three years as a junior.

In preparation for my first time playing for Miss Bee, I learned the piece "Malaguena" from the *Andalucia Suite* by Ernesto Lecuona. It is a very showy piece and one that takes precision, with very fast fingers using the entire keyboard. I was very proud of the way I had prepared for it, and as I played it for her I felt confident. When the last note was played I waited to hear the praise I felt I deserved.

I was mortified when she used the phrase "higgledy-piggledy" to describe my playing. I vowed to never let that happen again.

We were assigned specific pieces to learn for the next time she came, going through all of Bach's Two-Part Inventions, some of the Three-Part Inventions, and various composers' sonatas and other works. For the final session we could pick any piece we wanted. I chose the Ballade in G Minor by Chopin. With the humiliation of the "Malaguena" fresh in my mind I worked that piece to the bone, putting everything I had into it. When I finished playing it for Miss Bee, I sat at the piano, almost afraid to look at her, waiting to hear her comments.

There was complete silence for a moment. I couldn't move. Finally she spoke.

"I have nothing to change; that was well done."

Coming from her that was the highest praise, and it was a proud moment for me. She was a hard taskmaster, but working to her standards pushed me to be the best pianist I could be.

I had finished all my training and now had both my musical degrees. Life as a junior was settling into a routine.

It was 5 a.m. I awoke early on this particular day because it was my day to get up before the others to start the fire in the kitchen and begin cooking the breakfast porridge. I left my bed and made it up with the precision that had become second nature to me. After my usual wash at my stand, I began to get ready. I stood before the mirror and removed my nightcap.

Quite ridiculous, I thought as I put the cap back in its proper place in the nightstand. *What is it about hair that would be so sinful for even another Sister to see? Even a strand?* Never was our hair to be seen; even when we slept it had to be completely covered with the cap. I ran my fingers through my short hair that I, like all the nuns, had been cutting myself for years. It didn't feel sinful. Or worldly. And it most certainly didn't look beautiful with the lack of skills I had with a pair of scissors.

I sighed as I recognized the rebellious spirit in me yet again. More and more often I was bothered by what I considered to be petty rules, like this one. I was finding it harder and harder to just accept the rules. I

50

was fully aware that this was in direct opposition to the vow of obedience I had taken.

Attempting to put my bad attitude aside, I continued to get dressed, then sat on my chair to quickly pray my rosary. With that out of the way, I stood up and gave an automatic glance around my cell, making sure there would be nothing found wanting, before heading down to the kitchen.

I joined another junior Sister in the kitchen, and together we prepared breakfast. Working silently we got the fire going, put the porridge on to bubble, prepared the coffee and tea, and put out the bread and butter. At precisely 6 a.m. we rang the big bell, waking up the sleeping convent. We rang it again at 6:45 to announce Office, made sure all was well in the kitchen, and joined the Sisters in the chapel.

Following chapel, Mass, and breakfast, I had a few moments before my 9 a.m. class, so I went over to the academy and supervised the girls in tidying up their own areas. I always enjoyed any interaction with them. By 9 a.m. I was in the music house, ready for my first student.

The music house was a stone's throw from the convent, and it was where I was beginning to spend more and more time. I loved the music house, as I had spent hours and hours and hours there losing myself in my music while practicing for my degree. There were four pianos, each in a different room, and there was always someone either practicing or teaching in one of the rooms and oftentimes in all of them. Since I had completed my degrees, this was where I also began to give lessons to the academy students as well as to students that came in from the surrounding community.

As I began to listen to my first student of the day play her music, I allowed my mind to wander, reminiscing about all the hours I had practiced. While I would often struggle with the intensity of the schedule I had to keep then, I was now struggling with the lack of opportunity to play. Because I now held my degree in piano it wasn't deemed necessary for me to spend time practicing anymore. Just as composing music was considered a waste of time, so was playing piano frivolously. I missed playing and practicing.

With all those hours freed up, I was given more teaching responsibilities. Today was one of those days that would be long.

Not only had I risen at 5 a.m., but my time had to be flexible to accommodate that of my students. I knew from the schedule that I would again have to forgo my recreation time after lunch in order to teach. It was the only time I had to talk to other Sisters, and I really felt that I missed out when schedules clashed and I had to teach. I felt the familiar resentment creep into my heart. I was beginning to have less and less interaction with nuns, and more of my primary associates became my students.

I also knew that I would have to find time later in the day to say my prayers and Office on my own because my teaching responsibilities would overlap with the communal times. Once again I would go to the chapel alone. Not for the first time I wondered why they had to be said in the chapel and not in the music house or anywhere else in the convent for that matter. On rare occasions, if the weather permitted, I would be allowed to go outdoors to say them, but this didn't look like one of those days.

The long day finally came to an end. As I lay in bed, I wondered if it were just my imagination or if all the days felt long. As I drifted off to sleep, rules and regulations bounced around in my mind, not finding a place to settle and be comfortable.

One of the proudest accomplishments of St. Ursula's Academy was the glee club. It had a good history, a good reputation, and was still going strong, with students coming from all over the province to study music and sing in it. When I was asked to take it over from Mother Mary Herman, it was an honour.

There were between 90 and 115 girls in the main glee club, as well as smaller groups composed of grades 9 and 10 girls and girls from grades 11 and 12. There was also a select choir of 25 girls who were the elite of all the students. The select choir sang in three- and four-part harmony, singing complex pieces, from madrigals to compositions by Hindemith and other composers.

The glee club was renowned for its excellence, and it was no easy job to take that on. Keeping up the standard in performances throughout the year and winning at the annual Humboldt Festival was expected, and it took great effort on my part. I was not as confident as I should have been to begin with, but with hard work and my passion for excellence in music, the choir continued to excel.

My confidence was shaken one year when the choir was performing again at the Humboldt Festival. The girls had done a marvellous job and won all the classes. I was very proud of them but also thrilled for myself. I knew I had done my best, and it showed in the results that day.

I was at the Sisters' house in Humboldt after the festival and overheard two Sisters talking. They both shared the opinion that we had won at the festival only because of the past history of the glee club, not because of the hard work I had done with them. Somewhere inside me I recognized that for the lie that it was, but a bigger part of me believed what they had said, and it brought my confidence down. For many years I carried that lack of confidence with me in my teaching, regardless of how often my students won top honours across the province.

The two greatest events in history, Christmas and Easter, were times of reverence, joy, and awe in the convent. Christmas was a beautiful celebration, focused of course on the birth of Jesus as well as his mother Mary. During Advent, which begins on the fourth Sunday before Christmas, we were not allowed to receive any mail; it would be saved and given to us on Christmas Day, making the day even more special.

It was Christmas Eve again. As I prepared for my part in the upcoming hours, I remembered back to my first Christmas in the convent.

I had been a postulant for just over three months, and everything was new, fresh, and exciting. We had not received any mail since Advent had begun, and now on Christmas Eve we were instructed to go to bed immediately after dinner. That wasn't easy for me. This was my first Christmas as a nun, and I was excited for that night's midnight Mass, my first in the convent. There couldn't be a holier or more reverent place to celebrate such a momentous occasion. Nonetheless, I did as I was told, went to bed early, and surprisingly even managed to fall asleep.

I was woken up around 11 p.m. by the most beautiful sound I had ever heard, a choir of angelic proportions. The song they were singing was one I had never before heard. "Gloria," the voices were singing. "Gloria, Gloria!" They were heralding the arrival of Jesus' birth, and as I listened to the voices blending in beautiful harmonies, I never wanted it to end. I closed my eyes and basked in the joy and the miracle of Mary giving birth to a baby they would name Jesus.

While I couldn't know the unfamiliar music, my heart joined in the words, "Gloria! Gloria!"

All too soon it ended, and we all got out of bed and dressed for the midnight Mass.

I snapped out of my memory. Now, years later, I would be one of the ones privileged to sing in that heavenly choir, a heavenly choir that was in reality made up of only a few nuns. I was honoured to have been asked to sing this treasured number, as only those with voices worthy of carrying that tune were asked. The song originally came from the Sisters in Germany and was only sung on Christmas Eve.

As the hour grew close we gathered and began singing as we walked down the hallways. At each room we stopped, opened the door, and sang for a moment to wake those sleeping Sisters before moving on to the next room. There was such a reverence surrounding this song, waking the nuns up, and then proceeding to the chapel.

Mass that night was a beautiful and glorious reminder of the gift that we celebrated. The next morning was Christmas, and as such it was a feast day. We were allowed to sleep in a little and then to talk while we shared in a special breakfast. There was no Mass that morning, as we'd had one the previous night, so after breakfast we had our Office, which was followed by receiving our mail from home from the past four weeks. It was a wonderful time to feel the warmth of family.

On occasion we would receive a gift from home. It was automatically given to the Mother Superior, as holding on to anything would be worldly, and our vows kept us from indulging. What happened to those gifts was anybody's guess.

Easter was also special, although it wasn't all a celebration, considering that Jesus' death was commemorated that weekend as well as his resurrection. During Holy Week, the week before Easter, we had special prayers, and the Office for the last three days was sung. We prepared for weeks for this, practicing solos and pieces together.

Holy Thursday was considered a holiday, and we had salad for lunch to remember the bitter herbs that the Hebrews ate while waiting to leave

Egypt. Earlier in the day we had the washing of the feet, where Mother Superior washed twelve Sisters' feet in remembrance of Jesus washing the feet of his disciples at the last meal he shared with them before his death. I'm sure Jesus' job was much worse than Mother Superior's, as the Sisters made sure their feet were well scrubbed before the ceremonial washing. After our lunch we spent the afternoon in the chapel, preparing for Good Friday and Holy Saturday.

Good Friday was always a sombre day, very quiet with meagre meals, and Holy Saturday was spent preparing for the glorious Easter Sunday.

Easter Sunday morning Mass was wonderful, especially if the visiting priest could sing well. I have fond memories of one priest in particular, a Franciscan priest who sang elaborate arrangements with an incredible voice.

Three years passed, and I was faced with making my solemn vows. I didn't seem much more settled inside. After six years in the convent, I had expected much more of a content and peaceful spirit. I had not found the relationship with Jesus that I so desperately wanted, and in fact, as each year passed without the realization of my dream, I closed up a little more, growing harder inside. There were days when I felt as if I was sinking into a deep dark pit and there was a cover being pressed on me. I felt trapped.

A small part of me wondered if making my solemn vows, vows that were made for life, was a wise choice, but in reality I couldn't see any options.

It was the usual spring retreat, my last as a junior, and just weeks away from the ceremony where I was to say my solemn vows. I used this retreat to really look inward, pray, meditate, and make a decision that I knew would change my life one way or another. I knew what life would look like if I stayed; six years in the convent had made that perfectly clear. What I didn't know was what life would look like if I chose to leave.

I didn't really entertain serious thoughts of leaving, because I still wanted that relationship with the Lord. I still had some of that same desire that I had as a teenage girl for a love affair with Jesus; it had just gotten very muddied with the rules and regulations and petty day-to-day life in the convent.

The truth is, the more I thought about it, the more I realized that I really didn't know what else to do but take my final vows. I had no idea how to make it in the outside world, so what other choices were there for me?

I really wanted to be a saint. I realized that a saint only happened with the fulfilling of certain criteria and not until long after death, but it was the life of the person, a holy person, that would begin that phase, and I wanted to be that holy person. Even during that retreat, I fasted and prayed for that hope, truly wanting to work towards that. I wanted to serve Jesus as a slave; there was no other way I could think of to get near him than by following through with my solemn vows.

And so I came out of that spring retreat in 1960 having made the decision to take my solemn vows and belong to the Lord forever in St. Ursula's convent.

Indecision and Conflict

*Be merciful and gracious to me, O God, for man would trample
me or devour me; all day long the adversary oppresses me.*
Psalm 56:1

Belonging to the Lord forever. How I loved that thought, how it held
me together as I stood in front of the abbot that day in May 1960.
While on this earth, my forever would be here in the convent, but I
knew that following through on this decision would mean that my real
forever would be in heaven.

I stood there again with Sister Tarcisia beside me; she had been
beside me from the first day as we became postulants, then novices and
juniors. Now again we stood together, this time ready to profess our
solemn vows. The abbot addressed us and spoke of the vows we were
about to say, how our life would be one of constant sacrifice but deep
joy in our hearts. He spoke reverently of the vow of obedience, that
complete surrendering of our will to God and his will, and how his
desires would become our desires.

He admonished us to remember that our vow of chastity, while
renouncing marriage, was done in response to Jesus' love and to give
back to him our hearts and our lives as a gift.

With our vow of poverty, he told us, we would be giving up rights
of ownership to anything earthly and would vow to share all that we had

with our community, freeing us from obstacles that would stand in the way of our spiritual perfection.

Following his words, we knelt and joined in the formal prayers before lying prostrate before the Lord.

Once again I lay there covered with a black cloth to represent my old life and was reminded of my selfishness, my rebellious heart, and all my confusion. Earnest in my desire to overcome that selfishness and rebellion, I welcomed the cloth and the prayers that were being said over me and anticipated the removal so I could say my vows. The confusion never really left me, but I likened it to what any bride about to say her vows must feel. Isn't there always a bit of nervousness and fear with making a life decision like this? No more so than just before the vows are said, tying you to eternity in that moment. So as the prayers ended I accepted the confusion, content to let that work itself out as I lived a life obedient to Christ.

As the cloth was lifted, I stood in front of the abbot, ready to profess my vows. "Sister Michael of the Kingship of Christ," began the abbot, going on to ask me if I was willing to profess the vows of poverty, chastity, and obedience until death.

With all my heart, soul, mind, and spirit I answered, "I do."

Bowing my head as a new bride of Christ, I received a wreath of flowers placed on my head, followed by a plain gold wedding band that was put on the fourth finger of my left hand. The nervousness left, and relief took its place. It was done. I had made my vows, and now there was a peace about the decision.

Together Sister Tarcisia and I went and sat on the front pew while High Mass took place. Oh, the beautiful music, the singing of a High Mass! My heart was full.

The next day life at the convent continued much as it always had. I continued to teach piano and voice, lead the glee club and all its smaller groups, and participate in my share of the convent chores.

With all that I was involved in, my days were incredibly busy, and I continued to miss recreation time. Whenever there was a performance or music exams coming up, I would also be teaching or conducting in the evenings. But there were only a few weeks left of the school year, and then the academy would be empty. I was looking forward to a relaxed summer.

During that summer I began to rethink things. I thought about the struggles I had before making my vows. I desperately wanted to stay strong in my vows and keep my soul spotless. The more I thought about it, the more I saw one solution come to me over and over.

I asked to go to a different house in one of the communities close by. I was hoping that with more time, not just for recreation with the other Sisters, but also for my own quiet times to nurture my soul, I could keep my focus on God rather than on the busyness that the school year demanded from me at St. Ursula's.

At the end of summer I was told that my place was at the academy. They needed me for the music programs and as a convent mother. It was disappointing, but part of my vow of obedience was to accept the decision made, and once again I resolved to make it all work.

And so the fall started. In addition to all of my other work I was now also given the task of being a convent mother, in charge of a group of eight to ten girls. I would receive the girls' mail, checking it before giving it to them; make sure that their clothing was in order; and take complaints from other teachers if their schoolwork was not up to par.

Having relationships within the convent was not looked upon as healthy, and we were watched closely to make sure we didn't develop any "particular friendships." This fear of friendships went back to a very strong mother superior, who had served in the convent for seventeen years. It was unusual for a mother superior to be allowed to stay in one convent that long, and she left a big imprint on the community. One of her strong beliefs was that relationships of any kind would lead to "particular friendships," and that must be avoided at all costs. And so there was always an eye on us with regard to how we related to each other, not just to our students. As the years went by I began to notice that whenever I worked well with a Sister, she was invariably moved to another house in a nearby community.

I just couldn't understand why I was not allowed to get close to anyone, why I couldn't be trusted to have a normal and healthy friendship. My heart and soul yearned for relationship, and while I now wondered if Jesus and I would ever get close in the convent, I craved a connection with other people.

Because I am a very relational person, needing to belong, it was natural for me to invest in my girls' lives as a convent mother. We got along well, and I wanted to see them do the very best they could. Sometimes that meant getting involved in their private lives, with all the joys and the problems. As these girls were living apart from their families, and maybe because I knew the personal cost of that, I felt listening and getting involved was an important part of being a convent mother. I remembered how special my own relationship with my mother was, and while I didn't take the place of these girls' mothers, I had had an excellent example of how to love them, and I naturally shared that with them.

I also loved the girls I taught. They brought back fond memories of when I was a student at the academy. I found myself chatting with my students often, even though that was considered a frivolous thing to do; I just couldn't help myself.

It was not a wise thing, I suppose, to get involved with the girls, knowing it could cause problems with some of the Sisters. They saw the relationships as a problem, that I was too familiar with them. I would often be reprimanded by the mother superior. It began to wear on me that I could never establish a relationship and that small and petty things became large issues. I began to feel isolated and confined, as if there were invisible bars around me.

In the midst of all my personal struggles and the wars waging inside of me, I still found my peace with God. Saying the rosary each morning reminded me of the mysteries of our Lord and also of his gentle caring for us. Praying each hour to give God everything I thought, did, or said kept me focused, and the silence, when it surrounded me, was sweet, whether it was the regular day-to-day quiet or the Great Silence each night.

And so the months flowed into years. I buried myself in my work, teaching, and doing new things with the glee club, even going so far as cutting two records and selling them. We raised quite a sum of money from those records.

I came up with the idea to perform an opera. One of things I had so enjoyed, both as a student in the academy and as a nun in the convent, was the annual drama presentation, so I decided that combining both singing and drama would be a fun thing for the students to do. We chose Engelbert Humperdinck's full opera *Hansel and Gretel* (first created and performed by Humperdinck in 1893). It was a huge undertaking for us and involved all those in the artistic departments: music and drama, as well as visual arts for costuming and set design.

Together we created costumes and built scenery, including a candy house that had real cookies and candies on it. To make the gingerbread costumes, we had students lie down on paper. We drew around their bodies, using those patterns to sew the bodies of the gingerbread children out of brown fabric. We then sewed matching hoods and mittens to complete them. The preparing of all the details was almost as much fun as the performance itself.

Our first performance of the opera was in our newly constructed auditorium, but it wasn't all that large and therefore limited the amount of people that could attend. We were asked to repeat the drama, so we set about trying to find another venue. It became apparent that the only other option was St. Peter's College, the boys' academy thirty-five miles away. So it was that we bused all the girls there as well as all the costumes, scenery, and props. There were 1,800 schoolchildren in the audience, and as I played the score on the piano on the floor of the gym, they all sat around me. It was an exhilarating first opera to perform and one I would repeat two more times.

There were so many joys involved with the glee club and the academy, it wasn't a hardship to throw myself fully into performances and music festivals. In March 1963 I created the first Ursuline Academy music festival. Almost every girl involved in music took part, and it was a great success.

Having immersed myself in music and drama, my religious life started to recede into the background. September of 1963 marked ten years for me in the convent, and I went from being Sister Michael to Mother Michael. It didn't mean too much to me, as by this time I was only going through the expected motions of being a nun. Long gone were the days when I had a crush on Jesus and the days of expecting to spend all my time with him. The reality of what it took to be a nun was a greater disappointment each day.

I suppose it's surprising that I made it this far. We were not encouraged to have a relationship with Jesus or to read the Bible. Even though we prayed and meditated on certain Scriptures, studying the Bible and getting to know the Lord was simply not part of our days. I knew that Jesus had died for my sins, but I also knew that I had to do my part. So I was diligently fulfilling all my duties, as I thought that if I did those correctly and often enough I would get to heaven eventually—after, of course, spending time in purgatory suffering off the guilt that I'd not worked off yet at the time of my death. I never neglected to pray my family into heaven, to do penance for the dead, and to deprive myself of something to help them on their journey.

Yet it did become just motions, rituals that I felt had to be performed.

That year I began to notice cruelty in some of the nuns, words that were meant to be spiteful, remarks that cut and hurt others and me. I seemed to be targeted, and I was thought to have much more influence than I actually had among the girls and the Sisters. I was always under the watchful eye of someone, and the lack of trust was beginning to wear on me.

In the summer of 1964 I made a thirty-day retreat. It hit me how far I was from God and that everything I did spiritually had become nothing but habitual. My heart was not devoted to Christ, and I realized that the life I had expected to have as a nun was never going to happen. I would not have my dream realized, finding that relationship where he and I would spend countless hours together, where he would talk to me and love me. I was a disillusioned bride, sorely disappointed in this marriage, where I felt like I was the only participant.

I spoke to the retreat master about my problems, and he patiently listened to me with not a hint of criticism.

In one last attempt to remain true to my vows, I again requested that I be moved to another of our houses. I needed to get away from all the pressure I was feeling.

When the word came that I was not to be moved, I became obsessed with getting out of the situation and began to think of my options. It seemed like suicide was really my only way out, so I began to think of how I could accomplish that. Throwing myself in front of a fast-moving car seemed the only way to kill myself. Unfortunately I was too much of a coward to do that.

And so the school year began again without any change, except that I was getting more and more discouraged and desperate. I wasn't sure how I would get through the year. I no longer saw any point in praying. Everything I did was being watched very closely, and I now had to report to the mother superior for every fifteen minutes that I deviated from my schedule.

There was one bright spot, the beginnings of a friendship with Sister David. We worked together with the girls, and we found a way to talk without being overheard. We would go into the gym, walk to the far end of the floor, and bat around badminton birdies.

It was noticed, however, and I was accused of developing a "particular friendship." I couldn't believe what I was being accused of and denied it vehemently, but it was of no use.

I also became friends with Jenny, the mother of one of my students. She, too, was a teacher at the academy, and she sang in our select choir, which was highly unusual. She was the only one I shared my true feelings with, and she encouraged me to leave. Hearing her thoughts gave me courage, and the idea of leaving started to take root deep in my tired soul.

Things were changing in the Roman Catholic Church. The Second Vatican Council was meeting at this time, and there were changes beginning in order to bring the church up to date, adapting itself to meet the challenging conditions of modern times. Parts of Mass would be done in English rather than Latin, and in convents habits were being modified and the rules surrounding being in public were loosening. In fact, nuns were being allowed to visit their families for the first time.

I was allowed to go and visit my parents, who were now living in Victoria, British Columbia. Mother Superior would be accompanying me for part of the way, but I would be going the last part on my own. I was still not allowed to stay overnight at my parents but was under strict orders to sleep at a nearby convent, which was fine with me. I was just thrilled to be seeing my mother again.

A few weeks after returning to the convent I was called to the mother superior's office and asked why I had lied about sleeping at the convent. I replied that I hadn't lied, that I had slept at the convent, but she wouldn't hear a word I said. She told me that my mother had written to my brother, telling him that I slept at home, and he in turn told the nuns, who then told the superior.

Eventually it was discovered, although too late to help me, that my mother had written words to the effect that she hoped I would be able to sleep at home. I was now labeled a liar on top of everything else, and it was the turning point for me. I finally made up my mind.

I had to leave.

I would leave the only life I knew as an adult. I would willingly walk away from my dream, what I thought was my destiny.

Since I was fourteen years old my entire identity had been wrapped up in St. Ursula's Academy and then the convent. Leaving would mean many souls would have to wait longer to get into heaven, and my own would be damned. It was a heavy burden, knowing the disappointment I would be to my family. But staying was just no longer possible, and risking my eternal life was something I would have to learn to live with. I was so desperate to get out that I was willing to risk the very thing I had been working so hard for.

Leaving became my only hope for sanity, and so I prepared to break the vows that I had made.

A Midnight Escape to Freedom

Therefore am I troubled and terrified at His presence;
when I consider, I am in dread and afraid of Him.
For God has made my heart faint, timid, and broken,
and the Almighty has terrified me, Because I was not cut off
before the darkness [of these woes befell me], neither has He
covered the thick darkness from my face.
Job 23:15-17

The decision made, I became obsessed, and it didn't take long to make it happen. The glee club had a concert two days from then, and leaving before we performed was just not an option. I just couldn't let the girls down. I planned to leave after the concert, after I'd settled the girls in for the night.

Jenny, the gym teacher I had become friendly with, promised to leave some clothes for me in the change room and to take a note to my brother Hubert, telling him of my plans. The night of my departure I would head to her home and take refuge with her and her husband. That was as far as I could plan. I simply had to get out, and I could only hope and pray the rest would fall into place as it happened.

Two days doesn't sound like a very long time to wait, but it felt like forever. Each minute seemed like an hour and each hour like a day. I was strung so tightly it felt like a simple touch would shatter me.

For two days I walked around in a state of complete nervousness. I was jumpy and scared to death. I looked carefully into the faces of the other Sisters, checking to see if they were reflecting what they saw in mine.

My mind raced. What if I was found out? What if I didn't have the courage? What if the clothes weren't there? What if?…What if?…What if? There were millions of questions in my mind, so much uncertainty, no path to follow. I had a small plan, but how was I to know if I could actually follow through on it or if it would work? While I suppose I had a rebellious spirit, escaping from a convent was not something I had even considered up to this point.

As much as I told myself I didn't need to think about my eternal security, it was weighing excruciatingly heavy on my heart. I knew that when I left the convent without being officially released from my vows, I would be automatically excommunicated from the Roman Catholic Church. I also knew that excommunication meant that my soul was damned. There was no hope for eternity unless I received a dispensation from Rome. There was no way I could talk to Mother Superior; nor did I have any access to the abbot. And those were the only two ways to get to the authorities in Rome who held the power to free me from eternal damnation.

As those two days crawled by, I thought about nothing but getting away from the convent. Yet every time I thought about actually leaving and being free of this life, thoughts of my eternal destination worried my mind. I knew what it would cost for me to walk out the doors without a dispensation. Everything I had ever been taught, everything I embraced to be true, and everything I had lived for told me I wasn't just leaving life in the convent. Far worse, I would be leaving my hopes to one day be with the Lord. By leaving, I would in effect be choosing to walk away from the Lord. It never occurred to me that he might love me enough to walk through this with me and meet me on the other side.

And my desperation led me to take the risk, willing to change direction, from the pathway that would lead to heaven to the pathway that would take me to hell.

No matter what the consequences, there really wasn't a choice for me. But as the hour grew closer I did think there was a small chance that I might be released from my vows and thus establish myself in line for heaven again. I hung on to that last ray of hope and prepared to see if I could leave and maintain my salvation.

The night of the concert came. Just before I took my place to conduct, my brother arrived and asked to see me. I only had a minute, yet in that minute he did his best to talk me out of my decision. There was no changing my mind by that point, but I shared with him my small hope, my plan to talk to the priest after the concert, asking him to give me a dispensation.

Then it was time to begin the last thing I would accomplish at the convent, and I took my place in front of the girls. Sheer nerves got me through that evening. While it was bittersweet, the end couldn't come soon enough.

The priest, our chaplain, was in the audience, and I managed to get his attention as he was leaving. I asked to see him in the confessional, where what I told him would have to be kept confidential. If I talked to him in the auditorium, he wasn't bound to secrecy, and secrecy was crucial for my plans. I couldn't risk him telling any of the Sisters or, heaven forbid, Mother Superior that I was running away.

Sitting there in the confessional I poured out my heart, telling the priest my plans to leave and asking to be released from my vows. My heart was heavy when he told me that the abbot was away and I would have to wait to see him. I replied that I couldn't do that, and he told me that there was nothing more he could do for me.

I left the confessional with the knowledge that when I walked away from St. Ursula's that night my sins would no longer be covered and heaven would not be mine for the taking. After my eleven years of service, of work and devotion, God would turn his back on me as fast as I was turning my back on the convent. And as much as I told myself I wasn't leaving the church, only the convent, because of my actions the church had to leave me. Until the day that Rome granted a dispensation, which would lift my excommunication and return me to the path to heaven, I would be lost to God.

I never once wondered at a God who would make a choice to cut me out of his plans so ruthlessly; I believed that this was the way it had to be. So I prepared myself as best as I could to accept damnation for what I was about to do.

The auditorium was empty, the public gone home, and I walked up the stairs to the top floor of the academy, where I would tuck my girls into bed one last time. That process always took the better part of an hour. Then I quietly crept back down those stairs and across to the change rooms, where I found the promised clothing.

My cell was also on the third floor of the academy, in a passageway that connected the convent to the academy. Curtains separated me from the walkway, giving me privacy. I was never more thankful than this night that I had my own space and there were no other nuns close by. It gave me the courage to continue.

As I looked over my cell, I made sure that everything was in place and tidy, concerned that if there was anything amiss, the Sisters would talk badly about me. That still mattered to me.

As I was making my final inspection I heard someone coming. I hurriedly slipped out of my cell, crept down the hallway, and quietly entered the girls' bathroom. There I went in the furthest stall, locked the door, and stood on the toilet so that if someone looked under the door I wouldn't be visible.

Sure enough, I heard the door open, and Mother Patricia, a Sister I dearly cared about, called out my name. I didn't move a muscle, holding myself as still as possible, standing on that toilet. I was saddened to hurt her by not answering her, but I just couldn't take any more. I was pretty sure she knew I was there, but after a few minutes I heard the door close and I knew she was gone.

My heart was ready to beat right out of my chest as I waited a length of time that I thought would be safe. Then I changed into clothes that were as foreign to me as the world. Pants! I, a nun still in the convent, was now wearing pants! And my head was uncovered for the first time in over eleven years.

Very carefully I tiptoed back to my cell and hung up my habit for the last time. There was no turning back as I walked down the stairs and across to the gym. I chose to make my escape through the gym, as it was the farthest building away from the convent and deserted at this time of night. The likelihood of being discovered there seemed less to me. I moved a little faster, knowing that there should be no one around to hear me there.

I walked the length of the dark gym to the door at the farthest end and opened it. The cold and dark of a Saskatchewan December night hit me. My destination was the road, and beyond that I had only a vague idea of where Jenny and her family lived. To get to the road, however, I'd have to walk the length of three city blocks past St. Ursula's buildings.

I hugged the wall of the gymnasium, then the wall of the academy, staying in the shadows in case someone glanced out the window and spotted me. It was 10:30 in the evening by then, and most everyone should have been in bed, but I wasn't going to take any chances.

The last building to get past was the convent itself. Beyond that were a copse of trees that would cover me well, and just past those I knew I'd find the road.

Once on the road, I started heading in the direction that I thought Jenny lived, but in my state of mind I must have just wandered around aimlessly. Suddenly her husband showed up beside me in his car. Jenny had been waiting for me and worrying, so sent him to find me.

Once at Jenny's house I couldn't still my nerves. Any minute now I expected a knock at the door, a phone call, a demand for my return. I fell into bed expecting sleep to take over, not having slept much in the nights preceding this one. Sleep didn't come. Thoughts of being free warred with reminders of the cost. Something I had taken to be a surety, my place in heaven, was no longer to be.

The night stretched endlessly on. There were no knocks on the door in the middle of the night. No one came to find me. I was safe, but only physically. I knew that I couldn't be any further from safety spiritually. I was now on my own, completely alone.

I lay there going over everything in my mind. Eleven years earlier I had been an excited young woman with a simple dream. All I wanted was to meet Jesus, to sit at his feet and spend the rest of my life serving him.

Through my own doing, I now found myself in a strange bed in a world that I knew virtually nothing of. The dream of the eighteen-year-old lay shattered around me, and I tried to contemplate what my life would now look like, I began to weep.

The First Few Months on the Outside

I will be with you;
I will not fail you or forsake you.
Joshua 1:5

After an endless night I woke to a quiet house. My first thoughts were of freedom, that I was no longer in the convent. By now they would be noticing my absence and realizing what I had done.

Right on the heels of the feeling of freedom I felt the pain of disappointing so many people there, people I truly loved. I wondered who would take the glee club over and how the girls would react when they found out that I had left.

I got out of bed and out of habit made it up immediately. I dressed in the same clothing that Jenny had lent me and contemplated my day. I really had no plans beyond my escape. And even though I was "on the outside" I didn't feel all that free; there was so much torment inside me that I was unable to make sense of.

Alone in the house and constantly filled with tumultuous thoughts, I was startled when a telephone rang, a familiar sound to most but unfamiliar to me. Without stopping to think why, I picked it up, but I didn't say anything.

On the other end was Mother Superior. She addressed me by name, telling me to come back. I didn't know how she knew it was me, and

I didn't say anything as she continued to speak. She told me that they would send me to Quebec, where I could get help.

I knew exactly what she meant. I would be sent to an asylum there and treated as mentally ill. I suppose from their perspective, mental illness was the only explanation for what I'd done. Perhaps I wasn't emotionally healthy, but I knew I wasn't mentally ill, and there was no way I was going to allow them to send me away. I lowered the phone in silence.

When Jenny came home from school, she drove me the few miles to Humboldt, dropping me off at Hubert's place. The first plan that I made was to visit the abbot in Muenster. Hubert drove me there, and I tried to explain to the abbot what I had been going through and why I needed a dispensation.

He didn't listen to me or appreciate any of my circumstances or my perspective, repeatedly trying to convince me to go back to the convent. Once he realized that I wasn't changing my mind he reluctantly brought out the papers that I had to sign in order to ask for a release from my vows. Until it was granted, however, my lack of salvation was still non-negotiable.

Emotionally drained, I believed that the best thing for me was to get out of the area. So my brother gave me a railroad ticket to Vancouver; from there I would get on a bus and go to my parents in Victoria. I was so hopelessly ill-equipped to be on the outside that my sister had to loan me a coat that was appropriate for the cold Canadian winter as well as $300. It was painfully obvious that I had not made any plans or preparations for life outside the convent.

I got on the train for the long trip to Vancouver and used this time to rest and to think. It was not a restful trip, however, as the closer I got to my parents, the worse my nerves became. I knew my father would be grossly unhappy with me, and this scared me terribly. My mind went around and around, trying to visualize telling my dad the reasons for leaving the convent. I couldn't find any explanation that would have a positive outcome.

I knew my mother would welcome me with open arms and not judge me, but in some of those lonely hours on the train I couldn't help but wonder what she would feel in her own heart for me.

In Vancouver I hopped on a bus to Victoria. I arrived seven hours late due to a snowstorm. As I expected, my father was very upset that I had left the convent. Dad and I never did have much of a relationship, but it was still hard for me. I desperately wanted his love and affirmation as his child, and the way he treated me greatly affected how I saw God. Perhaps it was fitting to have my earthly father not pleased, as I knew for sure that God wasn't happy with me and was in fact ready to send me to hell.

Mom was glad to have me home, and I was pleased to be with her again. My sister Ann was living nearby and often had a calming effect on everyone, mediating between my parents and me.

Those first few days were very hard, and the tension was very high. Dad kept asking me to explain my decision and yet never tried to understand my answers. To be fair, my answers were likely very weak, as I was so confused about everything, and my father was as sure of everything as he had ever been. I was the one who had changed, not him.

Try to imagine the world in 1964. From the time I was fourteen, in 1949, I had been part of the day-to-day lives of the nuns, first as a student and then as a nun. Even though as a boarding school student we went home for holidays, my main shaping as a young woman came from the Sisters and the Catholic faith. I had never dated a boy, I had very little to do with fashion beyond costuming, hairstyles were foreign, and my life was just not of the world.

Now it was almost 1965. I had missed an entire decade and a half, the time of transition between the Second World War and the demand for freedom. In 1953 when I entered the convent, most mothers stayed home with their families, kept a tidy home, and doted on their men and their children. Now I entered a world where women had permanently joined the workforce and burned their bras. "Peace and love" was the theme of long-haired young people, and respect seemed to be a thing of the past. I found it difficult to understand the language that these bell-bottomed, flower-powered teenagers spoke, their slang like another language to me. Rock and roll replaced my classical and choir music, drugs were becoming prevalent, and sex was something no longer just for marriage. There were television sets in almost every living room, and every family owned a vehicle. Women were being encouraged to leave their "slavery" and work outside the home and dress more and more like men.

Noise and confusion had taken over what used to be my ordered and peaceful world. Even though I had chosen to leave and was excited to see and experience everything, it was still a shock.

In those first few days, Ann, Mom, and I went shopping for clothing, as I had nothing to wear. With no money left after coming to the west coast, I relied heavily on my family to help me.

The first thirty days out of the convent, while I was waiting for my dispensation from Rome, there were times when I could put the whole situation out of my mind with the beauty of the Christmas season that was now upon us. I had never lost my love of all the pageantry of the season, and in the convent nothing was as sacred and majestic as Christmas. The music alone was awe-inspiring. Being able to celebrate it surrounded by my family seemed almost perfect after all those years.

In January my sister Emm came to visit me, and we went shopping to try to fill in the many gaps in what I needed in the real world. We were in the lingerie section of Eaton's department store. No longer having to wear ill-fitting homemade cotton undergarments, I needed to choose panties, but as I looked at the rows and rows of different styles and colours, the whole thing was just too overwhelming. I was completely incapable of choosing my own underwear, and I burst into tears.

Emm took me to her doctor. He listened very gently as I told him what I had been going through. Just being able to share it with someone who didn't have any preconceived notions about me helped. I left his office feeling a small thread of hope, that I might be okay, that all I was feeling was completely normal. Of course that one-time visit was just a tiny Band-Aid on a wound that needed serious suturing, but it lifted me up and gave me the courage to keep looking forward.

I knew I couldn't keep relying on my family for everything, so I started to think about getting a job. There wasn't much I was qualified to do, but I excelled in cleaning, so I found a job as a maid in a motel. Being busy with work that I was comfortable with helped me get through each day. Cleaning was a natural thing for me and gave me the time and space I needed to think about what I should do next.

Music was what I really excelled at, what I had a passion to do, but all my training and experience was in the convent. I knew I was a good teacher but wasn't sure how to go about getting students of my own.

As the first month back at home came to a close, the papers came through for my excommunication in the Roman Catholic Church to be lifted. Rome had granted me a dispensation, and my standing in the church as well as in heaven was restored. I eagerly signed the papers, but that was the last I ever saw of them; I never received my copy of them. It didn't weigh heavy on my mind, however, as I felt a spiritual load lift off my shoulders.

I didn't go back to church, though, or at least not often. When I did go on occasion, I tried to pray, but I felt that my prayers bounced back to me unheard. It didn't surprise me; I must have been such a disappointment to God. If I couldn't find him while I devoted myself to him for eleven years in the convent, it was unlikely that he'd meet me once I pushed him aside. After a while, I just stopped going to church altogether, allowing that dream as well to lie shattered.

As life became more familiar to me, and I adjusted to my new reality, I decided to pursue my music. I phoned the conductor of the Victoria symphony, Werner Muller, and asked if there were any available jobs copying music. In the course of our conversation I shared with him that I had recently left the convent. He asked me to come in for an interview.

He was in the process of setting up the Victoria Conservatory of Music and was looking for someone to head the vocal department. In order to do that, however, I would need more training. Muller phoned his friend Ruzchena Herlinger in Montreal to see if she would agree to take me on as a student. To my astonishment she said yes. So it was that in March I found myself back on a train, only going east this time.

Performance and Depression

I am weary of my life and loathe it! I will give free expression to
my complaint; I will speak in the bitterness of my soul.
Job 10:1

I arrived in Montreal with very little money. Ms. Herlinger had arranged for me to live at a neighbour's apartment, and I began the process of learning to live on my own. It was lonely at times, but it was all such a new experience that I embraced every moment. I rented a sewing machine and began sewing clothes for myself; there was no way I could afford to buy anything, and I loved the whole process of creating something new.

Before I knew it I was immersed in music again, although this time it consisted solely of voice exercises. Every day for thirty minutes Ms. Herlinger would work with me, teaching me techniques that I needed to develop my voice. I learned things from her that I had never learned before and worked hard at my lessons. I was so focused on technique that in the four months I spent with her I only learned one or two actual songs.

I loved Montreal. I loved to go into the little boutique shops and look at the designer fashions. It was all so new to me and so enthralling. I just loved looking at the clothes and touching the fabrics, imagining myself wearing them. Once in a while I would try on an outfit and then sketch it while in the dressing room. Those designs came in handy later on when I was on stage and had to make my own costumes.

To help with my meagre budget I took a job with a babysitting service (I know, a nun becoming a nanny, who would have thought?). I babysat children in various homes and for wealthy families. Some I became friends with, others I refused to stay with when their children did nothing but fight. This was just a temporary job, as I knew that music was my future.

That spring Werner Muller was in Montreal doing some recordings. I sat in on some of them, and we chatted about my future. We both knew that at the age of twenty-nine I was too old to break in to the performing field as a professional. Werner suggested that I come back to Victoria for the summer and take a conducting class that he was teaching. In the fall he wanted me to go to Europe and visit different conservatories to see how they were set up and then come back to help him with the Victoria Conservatory of Music.

I eagerly agreed with this plan and so prepared myself to do that.

While I was excitedly preparing for the next step in my new career, things were not going very well back home in Victoria. My father had made a trip to Saskatchewan and met with the abbot, who told my father lies about me. My father chose to believe every word, refusing to give any credence whatsoever to anything I had told him. I was told that when I arrived back in Victoria I would not be welcome in my father's home. I would be allowed to stay one night, and then I had to move on.

There was no doubt that my father thoroughly disliked me, that he hadn't in fact wanted me from the beginning. As a child I only suspected that, but then one day when I was fifteen or sixteen I heard my mom and sister talking in the next room. They didn't know I was in the house, let alone within earshot, so they were speaking freely. That's when I heard my mother say that Dad had never wanted me, that he was very upset when he found out Mom was pregnant and even more so when I was a girl. My heart felt stabbed all over again that day.

Fifteen years later I still couldn't understand why my father disliked me so much, and I still wanted to please him. He was my father, and the place that he should have filled in my heart was a big hole that nothing else fit. It hurt when he wouldn't believe in me or give me the benefit of the doubt or see that I wouldn't lie to him. What shaky ground we might have been on in our relationship was now nonexistent. I was beyond hurt, and anger now began to fill that hole.

Even without a place to stay, I decided to go back to Victoria and pursue the plans for Europe and the conservatory. It all pointed to a very promising future and one that I knew I could be passionate about.

Finishing up my lessons and my job in Montreal, I took the train to Saskatoon. Jenny met me there, and together we drove to Victoria. She was in the process of moving there and was looking for a job, so we traveled together and stayed at her aunt's place in Victoria.

I was counting on borrowing the money to go to Europe from my dad. He had always been very generous with loaning money to my brothers and sisters, so I wasn't anticipating any problems. I was quite excited to go to Europe, knowing that this would be the first step of my future.

When I approached my dad, however, he turned me down. I could not believe that I would not be given the loan. Could my father possibly hate me that much? Perhaps it was his way of punishing me because I disgraced the family or because of the lies that had been told about me, but without money there was no chance of me going to Europe.

My hopes were dashed and with them my potential work with Werner. Another dream, albeit a relatively new one, lay shattered before me.

With no other choice left to me, I began looking for a job. I was living with Jenny at this time because I had no place else to go. Now that my hopes for the future were also gone, I stayed with her while I tried to find work. When Jenny found a teaching position in Ladysmith, ninety kilometres from Victoria, I went with her. I had purchased a piano before I went to Montreal, and this came with us into the small house we found to live in.

We made plans for Jenny's daughter to go to the local school, and I would teach her piano and voice. To make ends meet, I also sold beauty products, and through that I met another piano teacher. It was perfect timing for me when she had to move and gave me her students.

Things were relatively normal except for the fact that I was cut off from Mom. I phoned home quite regularly, but if Dad answered I would hang up. If Mom answered and Dad wasn't close by we could chat, but it was frustrating at best.

The following year I answered an advertisement for a music teacher at Queen Margaret's School in Duncan, about thirty kilometres closer to Victoria. After an interview I was offered the job. I taught piano to students from beginners to grade 5. I enjoyed the girls and had a good relationship with them. Music lessons were a nice change for the students in the loneliness of boarding school.

Teaching afforded me the opportunity to perform again. Each year the school joined with the boys' school at Shawnigan Lake and performed a musical. The first year I was there they planned to do *The Pirates of Penzance*. They were looking for girls to fill a role for a very high voice. I asked to audition and did the opening cadenza. I sang to the best of my ability and was rewarded at the end by a standing ovation from the cast.

The accompanist for the show was one of the directors of the summer shows at The Butchart Gardens in Victoria. Butchart Gardens is a fifty-five-acre floral display and a national historic site of Canada. With hundreds of thousands of people coming through each summer, one of their attractions was their summer entertainment program, performed four nights a week. When the accompanist asked me to audition for it, I jumped at the chance. It meant I would get to be on the stage, something I loved to do. I was cast in the major show and in Scottish Nights, singing along with Jock Dunbar, a well-known baritone of the 50s and 60s in Victoria. I had no idea what I was getting in to.

The first rehearsal was an eye-opener for me. Just two years out of the convent, I had a hard time with the vocabulary of the day. We opened the rehearsal with "The Rhythm of Life" from *Sweet Charity*, a modern musical that had just come out on Broadway in 1966. The song was pure rock and roll! The nun inside me was shocked, and I didn't think there was any hope of me learning it. I couldn't have moved any farther away from my roots in the convent. But the music stirred my soul, and with some extra help from the director with the dance moves, I did learn it and even enjoyed it. If the Sisters could have seen me, they would have been horrified.

They weren't the only ones. My mother came to see me perform one night and came backstage afterward to beg me to not continue performing. But of course I continued. Music, drama, and the stage were part of who I was.

I threw myself completely into those summer evenings at Butchart Gardens. Then I was asked by the owner to take her place as a hostess when she had back surgery. I would arrive at the Gardens at 5:30 p.m. and go to the private area, where a buffet was set up. My job was to mingle with the elite guests. I found myself in the exciting company of royalty, celebrities, and reporters for the elite.

It became obvious that I needed clothing very specific to this job, so my sewing machine began to hum. I used whatever fabric I could find inexpensively, and one of my dresses was actually made from drapery material. For that one, the pattern cost more than the fabric. To wear with each dress I found a short fur jacket in a thrift store that cost me a mere three dollars. I wore that jacket for years.

The shows were on Mondays, Wednesdays, and Fridays, and on Thursdays I joined Jock in the Scottish Nights, where I had several solos accompanied by Grace Timp.

At the end of my first summer there I received a scholarship from them for dancing lessons and to work with Grace on repertoire. Once a week I drove to Victoria, where I'd work with Grace during the day and then take dancing lessons in the early evening. Dancing was much more difficult for me, as I'd never done it before, so I had to work hard to master the routines. My efforts were rewarded the following summer when I found the dancing at the Gardens much easier.

Another show that I was asked to be part of was *Showboat*, and while playing Magnolia I met Shirley, another actor. She and I hit it off immediately and became close friends. Shirley was a Christian and never shied away from talking about her relationship with the Lord. As we grew closer she invited me to her monthly ladies' luncheons, called Women Aglow. There I listened as women sang, prayed, and spoke of the Lord and how they loved him and worshiped him. Every month I looked at these women, dressed so beautifully, full of all the right words, and couldn't help but be very critical of them. I thought they were just putting on a great Christian show, and I wondered what they were like when they were at home with their families and things weren't going well. Did they still sing praises and talk adoringly of God? I doubted it, but that never stopped me from going with Shirley or really enjoying her friendship.

Very slowly I began to realize that the relationship I had with Jenny was not normal. Her husband had become involved with another woman while he was serving overseas in the air force, and he wanted a divorce. Jenny began to look to me as his replacement and became very controlling of me, very demanding and very jealous. I knew that things were not healthy, but I had no idea how to get out of the situation.

Again, my time at the convent didn't prepare me for any sort of relationship issue, which was probably why it took me so long to realize that the pseudo family I was part of was not a natural relationship. When I left the convent all I wanted was an ordinary life, a husband and children. The relationship with Jenny completely blindsided me.

After two years of teaching, we decided to move to Duncan. I didn't know how to get myself free of Jenny. I repeatedly tried to put distance between us, but she had a way about her that always drew me back to her. Often I wasn't even aware of being pulled back into the relationship. She would tell me who I could be friends with, where I could go, what I should be doing. I seemed helpless under her spell.

While I was struggling with all of this, I became involved with a married man who believed that having a girlfriend or mistress was perfectly normal. I knew this also wasn't a healthy relationship but did absolutely nothing to stop it. And of course I didn't let Jenny know about him, because I knew she wouldn't approve, so I was constantly lying and sneaking around, trying to meet my lover.

Both situations were taking their toll on me. It was as if I no longer had any control over my own life. It was a familiar feeling to me; it seemed that I just naturally fell into places where I gave away control. It was comfortable for a time because it was what I was used to from my father and then the convent. Yet eventually I would get in so deep that I could no longer see any options.

It was a Sunday afternoon, and Jenny and I had been invited to go on a hike with friends. I was looking forward to the excursion. When Jenny told me at the last minute that we weren't going after all, it was the final straw.

Tossed between two unhealthy and unnatural relationships, with both people expecting things from me that I no longer wanted to give but didn't know how to refuse, I could only see one way out. That was to just remove myself from the world. I seemed to get into one controlling situation after another. There was no place for me to go, no one to take me in.

I decided that sleeping pills would be the best way to go, and that Sunday afternoon I swallowed an entire bottle of them. Jenny found me shortly after I had taken them, though, and she gave me something that made throw up the pills. She persuaded me to stay alive. Once again, I allowed her that control and threw up so violently that I broke all the blood vessels in my face. I couldn't go to work for an entire week.

I was alive, but without the ability to change my circumstances. I was still with Jenny, still with the married man. In desperation and severely depressed, I went to see my doctor, an elderly Scotsman, who was everything I needed at the time. I told him much of what I was going through, with the exception of my relationship with the married man, because he was a friend of his.

He suggested that I see a psychiatrist, but after one visit I felt I could not trust him, so I stopped going. Instead I kept having appointments with my doctor, and he listened very patiently to me. As well as listening, he prescribed the antidepressant Nardil, but I experienced side effects with it. Eventually my doctor admitted me to the hospital so that I could be put on proper drug therapy and monitored closely.

That first week in the hospital was horrible. I couldn't stand to have anyone in the room; the noise of their breathing hurt my head. The only person I would allow in the room was a very good friend who was a male nurse. I didn't want to see anyone else. I was afraid of what people would think; I didn't know what to say to them or how to handle relationships, even just the normal ones.

The medication was regulated, and slowly I learned how to be around people again. I felt like a zombie, though. I had no feelings, no emotions. The doctor explained that I had gone on adrenaline for so long that I had caused a chemical imbalance in my body. It would take some time for this to heal, but he felt confident that if I stayed on my medication I could be discharged from the hospital.

Coming out of the hospital sixteen days after I was admitted, I had no place to go but back to Jenny's. I didn't have the courage or strength to do anything to break away from either her or the married man, so I just coasted along in the same way I had before.

My brother Pete and his wife, Hilda, came to Victoria to visit my parents, and Ann used their visit as an excuse to try to get Dad to talk to me. We both hoped that there would be some healing, restoration, and forgiveness, but my father was not capable of loving me. Not before this visit, and not after. The only benefit from that visit was that Dad knew I was alive.

The following year, 1969, Dad became very ill, and the family was called in. My married friend and his wife drove me to the hospital to see him. He was still able to talk and spoke to my siblings and their families, yet hardly acknowledged me. Again Ann tried to make peace between us, but he wouldn't have anything to do with it.

A few days later, my father passed away. Suddenly all my dreams for a relationship with my dad were dashed. Somehow I would have to deal with the fact that my father simply had not loved me. How could a father not love his daughter? I agonized over the loss of that relationship. I stuffed down the feelings of not being adequate for him. I shed no tears for him at his funeral, as I was too angry to really care that he had died. Of course it was all borne out of the hurt inside me, but anger felt much better than the pain of being unwanted.

A chapter in my life had closed, but the hurt, confusion, and pain of my father's actions would go with me for the next forty years.

A Man, Two Hippies, and a Shipwreck

*But the Lord sent out a great wind upon the sea, and there was a
violent tempest on the sea so that the ship was about to be broken.*
Jonah 1:4

There are things that eleven years in a convent just can't prepare a
woman for. I came to realize that I was a hopeless judge of character.
Or perhaps it was just that I had not been exposed as an adult to people
in a normal and healthy environment, so I couldn't distinguish good
relationships from bad relationships. As people came into my life, I just
allowed things to happen and then often found myself in situations out
of my control and understanding. I never knew what it felt like to be
loved by my father and hadn't been around any healthy male-female
relationships, so I suppose it made sense that I had no direction.

The year after my father died I was involved with the Duncan
Musical Theatre. We were in the process of trying to cast a home-grown
musical, but it was rather pathetic.

We were having one of our regular meetings when a man came into
the room. He was about six feet tall with light brown hair and blue-grey
eyes. He carried himself very well, came across as very distinguished, and
he caught my attention from the moment he walked into the room.

This very good-looking man introduced himself as Bob Cooke. He
was representing the arts council and looking for support and assistance

from us. He was himself an actor and an artist, having been under contract with Columbia Pictures in Los Angeles as well as with the CBC in Vancouver. As the meeting progressed, it became apparent that Bob had an entrepreneurial spirit, and he all but burst with ideas.

I felt myself drawn to him. By the end of the evening he had agreed to direct *The Sound of Music* with me and also managed to convince me to form our own touring company.

Together with one other woman, we began work on putting together a show that consisted of excerpts from fifteen musicals. When it was ready to take to the road, it was really very good. But good wasn't enough for us to make much money doing it; the best night we had was a performance that earned us enough to buy a Chinese dinner afterward. It was a highlight for us.

Bob was a charmer, and I fell completely under his spell right from the first night we met. In the following days, weeks, and months, my feelings grew of their own accord. Once again I felt like I had no choice but to follow another person. Bob always lived life on the edge, full of dreams and plans. Very spontaneous, he would go off on adventures on the spur of the moment, and he was very exciting to be around. He had incredible ideas and wasn't bound by rules and regulations, and it didn't take long for me to get swept up into those ideas and into his life.

As Bob and I worked closely together on the musical, we began to form a close bond. Within that relationship, he shared his story with me, which I found tragic. He was born in England to wealthy parents, but when his father sold the family home for a pittance shortly after Bob's birth, their family was out on the street. Bob's mom had to go back to work, while his dad struggled continuously with depression (he had been gassed in World War I, thought to be a contributing factor).

When Bob was only four years old he was sent off to boarding school, which in itself would be traumatic. He was put on a train all by himself, and the experience was terrifying. In school, he was a poor boy in a rich world, and so he started living in a fantasy world, making up stories about his life to make himself appear better than he was. He developed many fears during his school years, and his only way to cope was to make up stories.

When World War II started, Bob wanted nothing more than to enlist, but he was too young, so he forged his parents' signature for consent and joined the Merchant Navy. He served there through the entire war, which only served to increase his fears. He had always dreamed of sailing, and reading books about sailing was something he couldn't get enough of.

He was everything I thought I wanted in a man. He was great fun, pleasant to everyone, and good company. He seemed to be genuinely interested in me, and by November of 1970 we were spending more and more time together, fast becoming a couple. I was still living with Jenny, and as I shared my story with Bob, he helped me plan a way to move out of her place. Once again I found myself planning an escape, but it was much easier this time, with Bob by my side.

One afternoon when Jenny was at work, we went to the house and packed all my things, and I moved in with my friend the nurse and his wife. When Jenny found out, she was terribly angry. It was difficult to be in the same city, as I couldn't completely avoid her; it just wasn't possible. But aside from cashing in a bond that we held together there were no serious repercussions, and I felt a huge load lift from my shoulders. When it became apparent that Bob and I were becoming serious, I also had the courage to get out of the relationship with my married friend.

Things were looking like they would finally work out for me. I had a great man who shared many of my interests. I was teaching music at school and performing regularly, and life was constantly rich and rewarding and exciting.

I wasn't completely blind to Bob's faults. I could see that sometimes he had money and sometimes he was completely destitute, that he wasn't always reliable. He needed someone to keep him on track and focused on whatever job he was currently doing. But I also knew how imperfect I was and that he was pretty typical for an artist. I saw nothing in him that would warn me to run away from him.

In January Bob and I drove down to San Francisco, where Bob had spent a lot of time. He loved it for the sailing and the artists' lifestyle. He wanted to share the city he loved with me, and I was excited to be part of it all. He took me to stay in the St. Francis Hotel, the grande dame of

San Francisco's historical hotels. It was overwhelmingly wonderful with its rich history dating back to the turn of the century. The high ceilings, the unique woodwork, and the elegance made me stare in awe.

One evening Bob took me to a special restaurant downtown. It was all thrilling for me, so new! When he asked the waiter for a piece of paper and a pen, I had no idea what he was doing. There at the table he filled the paper with words before handing it to me.

As I read what he had written, I realized that these were wedding vows. I looked at him with a bit of confusion, and he explained that he was asking me to marry him. Excited, I said yes, and my heart felt full and happy. I was getting married! We didn't talk about the details right then, but my mind was already full of plans for the dress, the party, the wonderful and exciting life we would share together.

After dinner we walked down to Fisherman's Wharf, where he bought me a ring made of braided gold and elephant hair. This symbolized great strength and purity, he told me, and as he slipped it on my finger, I went along with the magic of an unconventional engagement ring.

To say I was slightly taken aback by his next words would be an understatement. As he held the hand that now had the ring on it, he declared us to be married.

It wasn't what I had expected. I presumed that we would go back home and begin planning a wedding. I wanted the church, the white dress, the majestic and glorious music as I came down the aisle. While it was exciting to be in San Francisco and I was thrilled to have Bob as my "husband," there was a part of my heart that was disappointed. I brushed that aside quite easily, however, as I was more than willing to take what I could get. And if a braided gold and elephant hair band at Fisherman's Wharf was what was being offered, I was accepting.

Back in Duncan I continued to teach and Bob did occasional jobs. He really was an amazing artist, both in painting and in sketching; he could draw likenesses of people with just a few strokes. I was constantly amazed at what he could do and then amazed at how he could let it all just drop off again.

As the winter turned into spring, Bob continued to read everything he could get his hands on about sailing. Being back in San Francisco had stirred up the passion to sail again, and he began talking about buying a boat and taking a trip together. A few years earlier he had read Tom Neale's book *An Island to Oneself.* Neale tells in great detail his story of living in solitude for several years on an island in the centre of the Pacific Ocean. He found the island of Suvarov and survived there, 200 miles from the nearest inhabited island.

Intrigued and wanting to be part of Bob's world, I read the book as well. Reading how Neale lived, survived, and thrived on a gorgeous island, I was mesmerized. Bob began talking about taking the same journey and living the same life that Neale had some ten years earlier, and I couldn't help but feel his excitement after reading Neale's story. I could imagine myself living an exotic life like that. Together we went through the book again, devouring the details and looking at them as if it were us on that island.

The island is actually an atoll, a ring-shaped reef formed of coral nearly enclosing a lagoon. Inside the lagoon there are about twenty-five islets, but only five of them are more than half a mile long, with Anchorage being the largest. Several groups of people had lived there over the years, with the most notable being "coast watchers" during the Second World War, a group of men who kept watch for ships or aircraft. When Neale first moved there in 1952, he fixed up the remains of the buildings, living there until 1964, when he left the island permanently.

It was now 1971, less than seven years after Neale had left Suvarov, and we could not stop thinking about the island. As typical for Bob, he took the idea and barrelled forward with it, starting to talk about acquiring a sailboat and how we would stock provisions for a six-month voyage. It wouldn't take us six months to sail there, but the plan was to go to the island to look around and see what we would need. We didn't know if any of the buildings would still be there or what had survived the years (tropical storms can do serious damage). From there we would go to Auckland Bay in New Zealand, where we had access to a home to live in. There we would restock our provisions before going to the island to live.

Bob and I were kindred spirits in that we both were rebellious and impetuous. He filled the need that I had for excitement. We were bored easily by the humdrum of daily life and were always looking for the next adventure. In reality, we both felt that we needed to keep running, to keep one step ahead. I never stopped long enough to discover what it was I was trying to stay ahead of. The idea of living on a deserted island appeared to fill our longing to get away, and so we began to work towards that goal.

Embracing the whole idea, we became real hippies, ready to live on a deserted island. Bob even grew a beard. We found a sailboat, a beautiful twenty-seven-foot (thirty-four-foot overall) Sea Bird yawl. Its beauty was there in the design, but at the time we found it, it was in very rough shape. It was a derelict boat, having sunk due to neglect, but when we had it lifted up and taken to the marine, the engineer looked it over and told us that the hull was basically sound. For $1,000 we became its proud owners and began the hard work of fixing it up. We named it *Cantata*, which means a story told without actions, scenery, or costumes.

The Sea Bird yawl is a boat built on the design of Thomas Day and C. G. Mowers. Day was the editor of the *Rudder* magazine in the late 19th and early 20th century. His passion was to create a sportsman yacht using a simple design that could be built and sailed by the average middle-class man. He based his design on the vee-bottomed workboat and promoted it as a new kind of cruising vessel, one that would float like a seabird at rest rather than ploughing through the water like the yachts of the day.

Cantata was a typical Sea Bird yawl, not exceptionally pretty and very functional. It didn't have a cockpit, just planks around the footwell. The cabin below, however, had unusual height and was quite roomy, being eight feet in width. Coming down the stairs there was a single bunk to the right and another straight ahead that curved with the bow of the boat. To the left was the "kitchen," a small stove and a sink with a table bolted next to it. All along the sides of the cabin above the bunks and kitchen, as well as under the bunks and in the head where the toilet used to be (we had taken it out to give us more storage), were storage cupboards. There were two portholes on each side that gave us light and of course a bit of a view when we were in the cabin. I couldn't wait to make curtains and start fixing it up.

90

Bob and I moved into a cottage close to where the boat was moored and began preparing for our voyage. Money was tight, but Bob did some painting and held a show, which brought in some money, and I borrowed $1,000 from my brother against the inheritance that I would be receiving from my father's estate. Along with cleaning up and painting the boat, I made curtains for the cabin and bought bedding and necessities. I prepared food as well, canning many jars of chicken and vegetables, each jar a complete meal for us. I also prepared quarts of fruit, bought canned goods, and sewed waterproof bags for the books and music we were taking.

In Neale's book he talked about two cats he brought with him to the island, and we decided that we, too, needed a cat. We found a lovely tomcat that had an equally lovely sister. Sinbad and Singood adjusted to life on the boat very quickly.

While we were working on the details of *Cantata*, we often took it out, and I learned hands-on everything there was to learn about sailing. Our plan was for me to finish out the teaching year and then set sail. But there was one more thing that we both felt that had to be done before we took the journey. Having a baby while on a deserted island was just not something we could take a chance on.

I realized the permanence of having a tubal ligation and how it would end another of my dreams. Yet it seemed to be the only smart thing to do. With the adventure of a lifetime waiting for me, I gladly underwent the procedure and gave up the dream of motherhood.

While I was recuperating, Bob arrived at the hospital one evening with bad news. *Cantata* had been rammed by a fishing vessel and had a hole in its side just above the waterline. While it was terrible news, we were thankful that the hole was not lower, or the boat would have sunk!

When I was released from the hospital we took the boat to a small bay close by and tied it to one of the pilings. That very night there was an extremely low tide, and it went over on its side in the mud, causing the planking on the side to separate.

We were devastated, and I wondered why all this was happening. But there was no turning back. I pushed up my sleeves and prepared to do whatever was needed to fix our *Cantata*. Bob had a temporary job doing some sketching and painting, earning much-needed money, so fixing up the boat was up to me. I took out all the old caulking and replaced it, often lying in the mud to do it. I was happy to do so.

All of this caused a delay in our departure. By the time we had it ready to go it was already the end of August.

Shirley and her husband, Graham, were not happy to see me take on this challenge. I'm sure they hoped that all these setbacks would mean that we would give up our dream. They accepted Bob as he was, but they knew he wasn't stable, and they were afraid that I would be abandoned in some far-off place. I wouldn't listen to anything against him, and I stubbornly followed him wherever he led us.

We packed everything up and prepared to begin our journey. There was only one thing left to do before we could take off to the seas. We had to take *Cantata* to Nanaimo, where it would be taken out of the water, have a small leak repaired and one final inspection to make sure it was seaworthy, and be given a coat of red ocher paint on the hull to protect it from tropical insects.

It was approximately a three-hour boat ride from Parksville, where we had the boat moored, to Nanaimo, and we headed out, excited to be leaving the world behind us.

A Life-Altering Accident

What is man that You are mindful of him, and the son of
[earthborn] man that You care for him?
Psalm 8:4

Twenty-four hours later we watched as the *Cantata* burst apart as it was hurled against the rocks on the coast of Hornby Island. I felt the impact of each blow right to my heart. Our dream lay in pieces in the water.

We watched the drama unfold on strange shores with people we had only just met. We were exhausted from fighting the storm all night and day. I was weak from throwing up so much, my stomach still filled with pain, and now as I sat there sobbing I had no idea what we were going to do.

A crowd of people appeared around us. With no choice, I dried my eyes and stood up. It was decided that the boat should be unloaded quickly, so with a heavy heart I approached the boat and got on board. We began to unload our things, and those who had gathered formed a line and handed our gear from person to person. When we were done I looked at the beach, where almost all of our worldly goods were spread out. It would have been more than enough for our island, but seeing what little we owned, I couldn't even speak.

The people we had been visiting before the disaster invited us to spend the night, and we gratefully accepted. All our things were brought to their home, and we realized that the boat was not repairable and our dream was really and truly over.

The next morning it was painful to watch as Bob and some of the men dove down into the waters where our precious *Cantata* lay and stripped it of all the brass, the masts, the spars, etc. It broke my heart to see all my hard work come down to just pieces and parts. Even harder was selling our new suit of sails and all the parts of our boat, yet I knew this was a blessing, because we would really need the money now.

With no place to live and no jobs to go back to, all we had was that cash and our car, so we called Shirley and Graham. They invited us to come to their place while we regrouped. That's also when we became aware that the Coast Guard had been looking for us, so very quickly we called them and let them know what had happened.

Back in Duncan, we had to face the fact that we no longer had the rest of our lives planned out and were now without goals. It never occurred to us to stop for a bit and wonder why we actually wanted to be all by ourselves, secluded from everything we had ever known. Had I looked closely at myself at this time, I would have seen a pattern of running away from my problems. It would be another year before I would begin to understand the hand of God in the circumstances that I found myself in.

The first thing we did was begin to look for a studio where Bob and I could both get back to doing what we knew best: music and art. It didn't take long to find a building. One side was already occupied by a couple who were running a paint store, and we arranged to lease the other side. Our financial situation was pretty grim, so we were happy to accept some help from the couple next to us in exchange for helping out in their store. After learning how to be a sailor and fix the hull of a boat I now found myself learning yet another new skill, mixing paint!

Our studio was one large room. Bob used half of it for his own studio and began painting in earnest, preparing for a show. I had sold my piano months earlier to buy a new suit of sail, so I had to borrow a piano in order to start teaching.

We now had a way to earn an income, but we knew we couldn't live with Shirley and Graham for much longer, so we began looking for a place of our own. We found some property about ten miles out of town and put a small down payment on it.

When we learned about a grocery store that was going to be torn down, we offered to help demolish it in exchange for the free lumber. With that we built a small tarpaper shack on our land, about twenty feet by twenty feet, and once again we settled into a life of sorts. It was a temporary home while we prepared our lot and planned a real house.

Bob had designed a beautiful six-sided one-storey house and ordered the lumber we needed cut to size. We used our car to pull out the stumps to clear the land and measured the area for our house very carefully. We had it all staked out before we hired someone to dig the footings. The day he came to dig the trenches we both had to go to work, but we felt confident that we had it marked well and that he understood what he was to do.

You can only imagine our horror when we came home at the end of the day to discover that there were trenches dug every which way except the way we needed them to be. Because he had disturbed the ground so much we knew we would not be able to follow our plan. We both sat down and cried. So many disappointments!

The very next day we were having coffee in a restaurant when Bob started designing a hip-roofed house on a napkin, working with the size of lumber we had already had cut. He explained to me that we could pour a concrete slab and build on that. The frames for the house would be built on the ground and then erected with a pulley and hoist.

We went back to our little shack and excitedly fleshed out his plans. There was no keeping Bob down. He just jumped right into the next adventure, and I was happy to jump right along with him.

As the weeks went by I began teaching music and Bob added art classes in Cowichan Lake to his schedule. On those days he would drop me off at the studio on the way to his art lessons and pick me up again at the end of his day on the way home.

One evening I waited all night for Bob to come and get me. He had no explanation, but I didn't push him for answers. It bothered me and created incredible tension within me, but there was no thought in my head whatsoever of leaving him or even questioning him. I had become the master of avoidance. Besides, I certainly wasn't perfect, and we were "married."

Shortly after that we were in Duncan when I began having severe stomach pains. Thinking that some food might help, we stopped for a bite to eat. On the way back to the car I doubled over in pain and then blacked out. Bob caught me and helped to lean me against a car. Two bystanders made a comment about me being drunk. Bob told them what had happened and asked them to hold me while he ran to get our car. He drove me to the doctor's office, where they rushed me onto a bed. I couldn't speak or use my hands.

After four hours, the doctor diagnosed a bleeding ulcer and sent me home with medication and a program that included a special diet along with the medication. I would never be cured but was told that I could manage the symptoms if I followed the doctor's instructions.

We finally were able to start our house. Except for hiring a professional for the wiring, we did all of the work ourselves. There was a small kitchen, dining area, and living room on the main floor, with a ladder that led to the loft that housed our bedroom. We had to bring our bedroom suite up there through the window. We had purchased the property next to us, as there was a pond and a big beautiful fir tree that we wanted. We had great plans for this property, planning being our go-to activity at all times.

It was the spring of 1972, and Bob and I were both teaching. Late one Tuesday evening one of my adult students offered to drive me home so that I didn't have to wait for Bob to come by later. It seemed like a good plan, and of course there was always the chance that he wouldn't even show up, so I accepted.

We were approximately halfway home when a red sports car came out of a side road and ploughed right into our right rear fender. We sheared off a sign post before going over a seventeen-foot bank, coming to rest between some trees in a field. I was not wearing a seatbelt, so I was tossed back and forth, hitting my head on the dashboard before being thrown out of the car, landing in a bed of poison ivy.

At the hospital I was patched up and put in a semi-private room. My legs were burning from the poison ivy, my nose was broken, and my head pounded incessantly. As the doctors checked me over in greater detail, they discovered that the whole bone structure in my head had been damaged, and they could not say for sure whether it would heal. What they could say for sure was that there was nothing they could do for me. Time would determine the extent of my healing. My five front teeth had also taken a huge hit, and again doctors were unsure as to the healing there.

For three days I lay in the hospital in agony before begging to be allowed to go home, as the noise in the hospital was more than I could handle. It was agreed that I could continue to recuperate at home as long as I wasn't left alone. We had neighbours I could stay with while Bob was at work, so it was arranged for me to go home.

My recuperation outside of the hospital only lasted a couple of days, however. Bob and I were having dinner with our neighbours when I began to feel ill, so we excused ourselves and went home early. By 10 p.m. my nose began to hemorrhage, and no matter what we did, we could not get the bleeding under control. Finally Bob insisted on taking me to the hospital ten miles away, and the only way I could keep the blood from getting everywhere was to let it run into a bucket.

For three hours they tried to stop the bleeding before finally contacting a specialist in Victoria who agreed to meet me at the hospital there. I was put in the back of an ambulance while Bob rode in the front. The ride was surreal as I drifted in and out of consciousness. Bob was having his own surreal adventure; the headlights on the ambulance went out, and Bob had to hold a spotlight out the window so the driver could see where to go.

In Victoria, it didn't take long for the specialist to stop the bleeding, and I was finally allowed to sleep. I was admitted and took that time to rest. Bob came to visit me the first few days, but then suddenly he stopped showing up. He hadn't told me of any plans that would keep him away, and I had no idea where he was or what was going on. When he finally came back to the hospital I questioned him on his whereabouts and what he had been doing.

His only response to me was "You don't want to know about it."

He was so right. I was getting used to his strange ways and quite comfortable with hiding my head in the sand, so I just let it go. I was glad that he was back and anxious to go home and to get well again. Ignoring things was so much easier than confrontation.

Back home again, things did not going well with my recovery, and I spent many, many hours and days with the neighbours while I tried to get well. The doctors could not give me any assurance that I would get any better; they had no idea if time would heal my injuries. They told me that with head trauma healing was often just a wait-and-see thing, so all I could do was stay at home and rest. I was told that the front teeth that were completely dead would eventually need root canals to keep them from rotting.

I was unable to sing at all, as the vibrations hurt my head too badly, so I couldn't work, and even though I received an insurance settlement from the accident, it all went to paying bills. Without any of my regular income, finances were tight, and the bills started to pile up. Unable to deal with it all, I simply stopped picking up the mail. I was too afraid of all the bills, and my response to fear and the unknown was to simply ignore it all and hide.

It wasn't just bills and Bob's idiosyncrasies that I hid from. In the seven years since leaving the convent, I had very successfully hidden myself from God. Or so I thought. There were times when I would automatically go to prayer, usually when I was in a crisis or facing a problem, but I never really expected an answer or even an acknowledgement from God. It was more of a ritual and a leftover habit from my convent days.

All around me I was burying things, from bills to problems to God; I was a master of avoidance. Fortunately for me, God is simply the Master.

Finding Jesus and Healing

I have blotted out like a thick cloud your transgressions, and like a cloud your sins. Return to Me, for I have redeemed you. Sing, O heavens, for the Lord has done it; shout, you depths of the earth.
Isaiah 44:22-23

Spring slowly turned into summer and then into fall. There was very little I could do except rest. My healing was slow, and sometimes it felt like there was no progress. I missed singing, I missed teaching, I missed being able to work on the house, which was still unfinished. Little more than a year earlier my life had seemed to be everything I could ever have wanted. Now I felt like I had nothing left.

Gone was my dream to find a relationship with Jesus. The dream to have my father love me was broken. The dream for motherhood was shattered, and living on a deserted tropical island would never become a reality.

At the time of the shipwreck, I had felt that all my dreams had been shattered. But then all the things that I had taken for granted, the things that were just normal, also seemed to crumble. I had an incurable ulcer, head trauma that caused me great pain, teeth that were dead, and I could no longer even think about fulfilling any dreams of music.

I was a modern-day Job. And I wasn't very happy about it. There was really nothing much left for me to lose in life, and I wallowed in self-pity. I spent hours just moping around, wondering how I had lost everything that was dear to me.

One thing that I did still have was a close friendship with Shirley. I wasn't much of a friend to her, as I could barely function, but she stood beside me the entire time.

It was Thanksgiving Sunday, October 8, 1972. Bob and I were having lunch with Shirley and Graham, and Graham asked Bob to go with him to Victoria that evening. Brian Rudd, an evangelist, was speaking, and he wanted to hear him. Without hesitation Bob said sure, he'd go along.

Somehow I knew this was a critical time for us, and even though there wasn't a crisis or a problem, I asked the Lord to let something happen. I had no idea what I was asking.

Our husbands arrived home at 10 p.m.

"Well?" I asked. "What happened?"

All Bob said was, "I'm going back tomorrow." Nothing else. No mention of what Brian spoke about, what the evening was like, nothing. Just that he was going back the next night.

I answered, "Well, you're not going alone."

Shirley and Graham didn't say a word; they just listened.

The next day was Thanksgiving Monday. It was October 9, 1972, a date that would be etched forever in my mind. Brian was speaking in a little apostolic church in Victoria, and the four of us went in and sat right in the middle. The music started, people began singing, and then Brian came out.

It seemed like everyone around us was praying. It was a little awkward being an outsider, not really understanding what was going on. Of course I had seen worship, praying, and even speaking in tongues when I had gone with Shirley to her Women's Aglow meetings, but I had always been skeptical. I spent more time wondering what those women were like when they were at home with screaming children and sullen husbands than I did examining the spiritual activity. And I certainly had never been to an evangelistic revival meeting before.

All at once Brian stopped his own prayers and pointed directly at me. I couldn't believe he was pointing at me, so I just sat there and squirmed. Besides, what was I supposed to do? Did he notice that I was the only one not praying? Was he going to pray for me? Point me out to everyone else?

Before I had enough time to think it through, his next words hit me. "The woman in the green dress." I looked down as if I didn't know what colour dress I was wearing; of course it was green. I looked back at him.

"Would you please come up? You have a nervous condition, a stomach problem."

I gasped, because of course I was still suffering from my ulcer, still taking medication to control it. He couldn't have known that. Without another thought I went forward.

He looked at me and spoke again. "You're a Catholic, aren't you?"

"I was," I responded.

"Do you believe that Jesus can heal you?"

"Yes." I didn't know where that came from. I didn't know if I really believed that Jesus could heal or that he would heal me, having almost completely left him behind in the convent. But I knew I had no choice but to answer yes and mean it with all my heart.

Brian prayed while I stood there, and the congregation joined him in praying. I didn't feel a thing. I'm not sure what I expected, but I didn't notice any changes in my body. After a while I went back to our pew. I never heard another word that was said the rest of the service.

On our way home the four of us decided to stop at a restaurant. As we sat in the booth looking at our menus, I turned to Shirley and said, "Hey, if I'm healed, I'm healed. Right? That means I can eat anything. Doesn't it?"

I ordered coffee, hot mince pie, and ice cream, all an absolute no-no for me, even with my medication. They would normally cause my ulcer to flare up enough to send me to hospital. Yet for some reason I felt confident in taunting God; like I said, if he'd really healed me, I'd know it very soon.

Shirley, Graham, and Bob just sat there, not knowing whether to yell at me or see what God might be doing. I thought at least one of them would have a fit at any second. Nonetheless, I was adamant about my choices, and when the coffee and food came, I thoroughly enjoyed myself, not leaving a drop or a morsel behind.

I waited, for either pain or healing. No pain surfaced, and when I got home I was prepared to throw out all my medication. Brian had told me to throw it all out, as I wouldn't need it anymore, but Bob insisted that I keep one bottle. Because he had been up with me many a night while I suffered, it seemed only fair that I give him that small comfort.

I went to bed, not knowing what the night would bring, half anticipating the excruciating pain to begin at any moment. Much to my surprise, that night I slept better than ever before. There was no pain; I needed no medication. There was simply no explanation except that I had been healed from my stomach ulcers. I was completely pain-free.

The next night we went back to that little church, and when the congregation began singing, I couldn't help but try to sing along. I loved singing, and I hadn't been able to for months, so I tentatively opened my mouth and let the first notes out. As the sound bounced around in my head, I realized that there was no pain. Just the day before, if I had attempted even a note, my head would've felt pierced. Now as I let a few sounds come out, there was no piercing pain, so I tried a few more.

When there was no pain, I raised my voice completely in song, singing louder, wondering if the vibrations would bring on the usual excruciating pain. Nothing happened, so I kept singing, louder and louder and continually pain-free.

We just couldn't ignore the fact that God had healed me of two very distinct and different medical problems, problems that were real and diagnosed. The next night we went back again and told Brian everything I had gone through, from the ulcers to the accident, and how God had healed me. His response was to ask me to sing the following night.

The next night I stood up in front of the people gathered there and told them my story, how God had healed me from my ulcer and my head injuries. And then I sang. What a joyous time that was, to sing for the Lord again!

After I was finished, Brian spoke, and after his message he asked if there was anyone in the congregation who would like to come forward and give their lives over to God. There was no hesitation for either Bob or myself as we both made our way forward. There at the front of this little church tucked away on a back street of Victoria, my life changed forever.

I repeated the words that Brian said, confessing that I was a sinner and acknowledging that Jesus had come to this earth and died for my sins. I admitted to being able to do nothing about my sin on my own and that I needed the Lord to come in and take over my life. I willingly surrendered everything I was to him. Beside me Bob was saying similar words.

What a difference there was for me immediately! I was on a new high, experiencing a completely new emotion. I had finally met the Lord. After all those years of desiring to have a love affair with Jesus, of tradition and ritual and obedience, of searching and trying and following, I suddenly met the author of it all. Jesus. All the head knowledge that I'd accumulated over my years in the church suddenly made its way to my heart, and the two became one thing. My salvation. I was thirty-seven years old, and I couldn't believe what had happened. I couldn't be more excited to finally live the life that I had envisioned as a teenager.

In my naive way, I expected that coming to know the Lord would mean that all our troubles would be over. After such a miraculous healing, surely life would finally become everything that I ever wanted it to be. I could sing again; I could eat again.

It wasn't long before we found out that life with God isn't trouble-free; it just means he is there to walk through it with you.

Now that we were Christians, we were faced with a dilemma. We were simply living together, not having ever legally married. When we had come back from San Francisco the year before we had told everyone we were married, but we weren't, and now we were faced with what God had to say about that.

Remember, this was the '70s, and while the world was singing about how all they needed was love, Christian morals didn't change to accommodate the world and the concept of free love. We were in a place of contradiction. We were believers and even giving our testimony at various churches. But we were still just living together, not having had a real commitment or ceremony in God's eyes.

We were both reading the Bible at this point, devouring it to find out what God had to say. I specifically searched for something that said that two people needed to go through a marriage ceremony but could find nothing definitive. It was strongly implied with Christ's first public miracle at the wedding feast at Cana, but I could find nothing that hit me over the head. Yet I was convicted that God really wanted us to be married the right way, and obeying him was becoming something that I really wanted to do. Yet I was afraid that if I pushed Bob on this detail he would take off, so once again I hid and said nothing to him.

I was scheduled to undergo a root canal on one of my five front teeth that were damaged in the accident. Those teeth were thought to be dead, and a root canal was needed so that they wouldn't rot. As I lay in the dentist's chair, he opened the tooth up to expose the roots and nerves, and I inadvertently took a breath through my mouth.

I felt pain! Excruciating, mind-numbing pain that almost sent me out of the chair. It took a minute to realize that dead teeth do not feel pain, and I was suddenly hit with the realization that God didn't just heal my ulcer and my head injury from my accident. He had, in fact, given me complete healing from nose to head to teeth. I can imagine him just smiling down, waiting for me to find out the extent of what he had done for me. And I couldn't help but smile back. With healthy teeth, no less!

We began attending church with Shirley and Graham, and I slowly began growing in the Lord. Our problems did not disappear, but I was beginning to see God's faithfulness through them.

We were to have only a few short months before my world crashed down again.

Losing Bob

Do not be afraid, neither be dismayed,
for the Lord your God is with you wherever you go.
Joshua 1:9

I was a new person. Outside and inside. Physically and spiritually. I had finally met the Lord Jesus Christ, the Saviour whom I had spent all those countless years trying to please. All the work I had done so faithfully to try to earn a place at his feet, I now realized, had been just rote, ritual, and routine. All Jesus wanted was my heart. There was nothing I could do on my own strength to earn my salvation; no amount of self-generated works would give me a place in heaven. In giving my heart and soul to him, I was completely and totally saved, and nothing more was required of me. Each morning I woke up in awe of that fact. From the love in my heart from him and for him, I was able to serve, to live as he directed.

With my complete physical healing, my world opened up again. I could sing, I could play piano, and I could work on our house again! As the fall continued, there was a new joy for me in everything. The world looked new from my renewed body, and there was hope everywhere I turned.

With great eagerness I joined Bob working on the house, being very determined to be in it by Christmas. We willingly and happily spent every moment we could on it. While we worked we would talk about the things we had read in the Bible. Bob couldn't get enough of reading it; any chance he got he would pick it up and read.

It was an exciting time for us. Our little home was shaping up beautifully, and working on it was a true labour of love. From the outside it looked like a doll's house, so cute and perfect. Inside it was lovely and cozy, with our beautiful fireplace that Bob built. I couldn't wait until the day that it would be functional and we could cozy up by our first wood fire.

We would often go to Shirley and Graham's for a meal. As soon as we walked in the door, Bob would head for the large family Bible that they had and just start reading. Our conversations around the table were about all the things we had learned as well as questions that our baby Christian hearts couldn't figure out on our own. I treasured the friendship even more now that we were all serving the same God.

As Christmas approached, Shirley invited us to spend the holidays with their family, but as much as we loved being with them, we could not be convinced to spend Christmas anywhere but in our little castle.

At this point we were heating our home with the cookstove, keeping a fire in the firebox at all times. It was fuelled by oil, and on December 23 we ordered more oil because our tank was getting low and we didn't want to run out over the holidays. We expected the oil truck to arrive before we had to leave for work, but it was running late that morning, and we had no choice but to leave a note for the driver and leave for the day.

When we came home in the evening, the house was cold and the fire in the cookstove was out. Very quickly we discovered that the oil had not stopped flowing from the tank to the stove, and now the firebox was full almost to the top with oil. We bailed and mopped up the oil as best we could, but it had seeped into the fire bricks, and they were saturated with oil. We soaked up as much oil as we could, thinking it would then be safe to light the stove.

Big mistake! The oil that saturated the bricks didn't burn but did smoke. And smoke and smoke and smoke. It became so bad that we couldn't even breathe in the house. There was no way we could stay there, so at 10 p.m. we drove to Shirley and Graham's. When Shirley saw us, she giggled and said, "I knew you would be spending Christmas with us."

It was the most wonderful Christmas. It was the first one where I felt like I was personally involved with the whole Christmas story. The meaning of Christ's birth washed over me in a new way as I realized that he would have come to earth as a baby and then willingly die even if it were only for me, to save me from my sins. It was intensely personal and genuine, that Christmas. It had always been a magical season for me, but this year the magic was in the spiritual implications of this little baby.

To make it absolutely perfect, it began snowing, and it snowed so much that the roads were closed. We didn't leave the house for a week. We spent our time playing games, cooking delicious meals, and even venturing outside to ski and toboggan when the sun came out.

It was a memory that would linger in my mind and heart when things began to change a few months later.

By the time Easter came around, things had settled down for us. We had not yet figured out what we should be doing about getting married, though, and it did weigh heavily on my mind and in my heart.

Easter Sunday came, and I was excited. I would be celebrating Easter as a new Christian, seeing the whole story unfold, being part of the resurrection of Christ that this Sunday would celebrate.

It did not happen as expected. Before the joy of the celebration came, Bob sat me down. He said he was leaving me.

Just like that, out of the blue, he told me he was leaving. He said he just needed some time to figure things out.

I was devastated. I did not see it coming. Had I been so wrapped up in my own life and my own passion for Christ that I missed some warning signs? Hadn't Bob been just as excited as I was about the Lord? What had happened that he would think this was a good decision?

Of course we weren't married, and this was in the seventies, so there were no repercussions for him. He could simply pack up and walk out the door as if he had been my roommate. Which is exactly what he did. I was helpless to stop him and could do nothing but watch him leave.

I was left dazed. The man who filled my every moment with excitement, who stood beside me as we both witnessed God moving in our hearts, the first man I had truly loved with everything I had, just walked out the door.

I had no idea why he felt he needed to leave. I desperately needed answers. I needed to know if it was something I had done, if there was a chance we could work this out, what he was going through and if I could help him. I tried calling him at the motel he was staying at, but he refused to talk to me.

Bob didn't want anything to do with me, our house, or the property. He appeared to just want his freedom from it all. As the days went by I did not feel like I could live there alone. It was still far from completed and quite remote, so I moved in temporarily with Shirley and Graham.

Within a few weeks, while I was trying to deal with the situation, to figure it all out, I heard that Bob was seeing another woman and was planning to marry her. I couldn't believe he could do this. Here I had been so careful not to pressure him into marriage, so careful not to scare him off, and he had not once mentioned marriage. Now, just weeks after walking out on me, he was getting married to someone else? My world was spinning. I was angry, and I needed answers.

Bob had a friend, "Ken," who had known him for years and years. I had met him several times, but those visits were odd. Bob never left me alone with Ken; he insisted on always being in the same room with us, no matter what. It seemed a bit off at the time, but I shrugged it off as one of Bob's little quirks. For all I knew, he didn't trust Ken or was jealous of him. I never discussed it with him.

When I was left with questions about Bob and this other woman, Ken's name came to mind, so I picked up the phone and called him. For the very first time, Ken and I had a conversation between just the two of us. I explained the situation.

There was a silence on the other end.

After a lengthy pause, he spoke, hesitantly. "Grace. There are some things you need to know about Bob. Bob is not exactly who you think he is.

"First of all, his name is not really *Bob*.

"Secondly, his mother is not dead as he told you, but alive and well in England.

108

"Bob also has a wife in Toronto, and I don't know if they are divorced or not, but I'm guessing that's why he was unable to marry you."

My head was reeling. Bob wasn't Bob? He had been married? How could he not have told me that? Why would he not mention that? And why would he tell me his mother was dead when she was very much alive? All I had were more questions, but Ken had more to tell me.

"I'm sorry, Grace, but Bob also has three children. I'm not sure if he has a criminal record, but it's not something I would rule out."

I could not believe my ears. Three children? Three children!

I hung up the phone and just sat, trying to digest everything Ken had told me. Bob. Not Bob. A wife. So that was why we got "married" in a restaurant and on the wharf in San Francisco and why he would never entertain the idea of us getting married. Three children? I couldn't help but think about how I so willingly gave up my dreams for a family for Bob's dream. I had believed we were both giving up the idea of parenthood. Never in my wildest dreams would I have thought he already was a father. And of three children!

I had not suspected a thing, and I was feeling more than a little foolish right then. It was all a lie; I had joined my life with a man who had based our relationship on lies.

And then I got even angrier. I thought of his new girlfriend, a woman I had once worked with, and knew that I had to save her from the heartache, pain, and anger that I was now experiencing. I phoned her brother and told him everything I had learned.

I don't know what her brother did with what I told him, but I know he put a stop to the whole wedding, even though the bride's family was already on their way from England. I suspect that he went to Bob and confronted him, because that same evening Bob disappeared.

I could not believe the life I had now, how everything I had believed, everything I had wanted and expected, was now a shambles. I continued to stay with Shirley and Graham, not simply because my house wasn't finished and too remote. I desperately needed to be with them, to find some help and comfort through what was happening.

Shirley and I both believed that we had not seen or heard the last of Bob. We knew that one day one of us would hear from him again. I took some comfort in that thought, each day still hoping there were reasons for him not telling me all this. Yet each day I also had to deal with the reality that he was gone, and I needed to go on with my life.

With no other means of support, I was forced each day to get out of bed and continue teaching my students. Once again my music became my constant.

Another couple weeks went by, and Shirley and I were out biking when I recklessly decided to head down a large hill. I had never ridden that fast in my life, and it felt like my heart was about to beat right out of my chest. We made it home and collapsed onto the kitchen chairs. My chest was hurting from trying to get adequate air into my lungs, and I sat there rubbing it. As my hand passed over I felt a lump that had not been there before, and I became terrified. Shirley and I immediately examined it, and we both thought it did not look good.

Due to the provincial music exams that my students were taking in Vancouver, I couldn't get to the doctor for a few days, but as soon as that was done, I made an appointment. The doctor took one look at it and sent me right to the hospital for exploratory surgery. While waiting on that bed for the surgery I couldn't help but feel sorry for myself. After all I had lost, it just wouldn't be fair to have to face something like cancer.

And so I prayed. I prayed that I wouldn't have cancer. I prayed that this was just a routine lump and I would be allowed to continue living. Even in my prayers my mind was going all over the place. If I had cancer, who would care for me? How would I earn a living? "Please, God. Please, God. You miraculously healed my entire body less than a year ago. You miraculously saved me and pulled me into a relationship with you. Was it only to die alone a year later? Do you not have something better for me? Please, God. Please."

I was never more relieved or thankful when I came out of the anaesthetic to hear that the lump was not malignant. I was fine! Praise God, he heard my prayers, and I was granted a new lease on life. With the thought that God was still on my side, still there with me every minute, I gathered new strength from him to keep on going.

It became very apparent that Bob was not coming back in the immediate future and also that I couldn't continue living with Shirley and Graham forever, so I began to look for a place of my own. I put our house and property up for sale and found a one-bedroom apartment. For the first time in my life I had my own place, and I found that I actually enjoyed setting up my own home.

That summer the conservatory in Victoria asked me to go to England to be the accompanist for their girls' choir, paying my way. As I had no ties to keep me at home and a change of scene would probably be a good idea, I agreed; it seemed like a great way to spend a summer.

It wasn't. Trouble began even before we left as one of the chaperones became ill. As another chaperone was getting off the plane, she broke her ankle. Before we even stepped foot in London I suddenly was not only the pianist but also a chaperone for the girls. Then, as we left London, our coach driver announced that he had never been north of London before and had no idea where to go. So with a map in hand, I became the navigator. The last straw was when the conductress, getting on in age, needed me to teach the girls the remaining songs that they hadn't learned before leaving Canada.

The trip was a nightmare beginning to end, and when we finally arrived back in Vancouver, I simply saw the girls off the plane, said goodbye, and left them. At that point I couldn't have cared less if they'd been stranded, I was so done with the trip.

Back home that fall I was finally able to sell our house and property. Even though there was no money left over from the sale, I was thankful that I didn't have to make the payments any more. Without Bob, I had let our rented space go, and now I found several rooms in what used to be a dentist's office with space to have two other teachers join me. I was kept busy teaching and accompanying students, which really helped with the loneliness that I constantly struggled with.

I was still going to church with Shirley and Graham as well as attending a weekly Bible study. I continually learned what it meant to rely on the Lord. While my walk was far from perfect, I knew that even when I fell back into old patterns, Jesus would be faithful to me. He would never walk away from me.

The year ended, and as we went into 1974 I continued to rely on God. Now that I had found a true faith, I was not going to let go.

My mother was now in her eighties and in a care home close by. I was fortunate to be able to spend time with her, reading the Bible with her and just visiting. One day in May we were reading the psalms, as we often did, both of us enjoying them and even more so when reading them together. We spoke of things of the Lord. It was a memorable day for me because the next day she passed away. I was so thankful to have had that time of reading and praying together.

Mom passed away on a Friday morning, and I had a recital scheduled for Sunday afternoon that there was no backing out of. I sang that recital with four of my sisters sitting in the front row, a rare treat for me. Afterwards I was obligated to put in a short appearance at the reception, and from there we went to the funeral home. My mother had asked me to sing a special song, "The Holy City," and so I did that for her.

The next day we all left for Saskatchewan, where the funeral was to be held. She had requested that I sing "The Holy City" there as well. The abbot, however, refused to allow that, and if it were not for my brother and brother-in-law, my mother would not have had her wish fulfilled. But they managed to convince the abbot to let me sing. After the Mass, my brother-in-law walked me back to the choir loft, and I sang that song to the best of my ability for my mother.

I stayed in Saskatchewan for a few days after the funeral. It was strange to be a visitor in a place that had been home for so long. I walked past our old home, which now had strangers living in it. Glancing up at the balcony I thought about how much had changed since I had done my little performances for my mother. Both my parents were now gone, and I was no longer a nun and no longer with Bob. I was all alone. Certainly not what I had expected when I was a little girl in that home.

I shrugged off the loneliness and reminded myself that I had my relationship with Jesus now, which was all I'd ever wanted as a teenager. I thought of all that had happened to me in this little town and decided that I needed to see the abbot. I needed to tell him that while I might have left the convent, I had now found peace in my relationship with God.

And so I boldly met with him and told him about my healings and how I had found Jesus. He didn't seem to care and gave me no response.

I had no idea what his thoughts were or if he even understood what I said. I just knew that God wanted me to share, and so I did.

I also went back to the convent. All the memories washed over me as I walked through the doors again. With each step the emotions were almost more than I could handle, reliving the happy days there and also some of the darkest days in my life. I realized that there was much beauty in the simplistic life I led there. There was a sense of serenity within those walls that sometimes I still longed for. I could hear the music in my head, the sound of pure voices raised to God, and for a moment I closed my eyes to let it wash over me. It sounded different to me now that I had a personal relationship with the one those songs were for. It was a comforting feeling.

I spent some time talking to the Sisters, many of whom were open, friendly, and willing to talk with me. As I left the convent that day I was pleased that I had had the opportunity to visit again.

When I returned home to Victoria, one of the teachers who shared my work space suggested that I go to Santa Barbara as a student in the Music Academy of the West's summer program. Having a small inheritance from my mother, I applied. I wasn't accepted as a student, but I was allowed to audit the classes, so I packed up and headed south.

This was a huge step for me professionally. The academy was performing the opera *Falstaff* that summer, and I became costume mistress for the production and taught many of the singers who were performing. One of those singers was a well-known performer from New York who would go on to sing at the White House, Carnegie Hall, and all across the world. We became friends and spent a fair bit of time together. By the end of the summer she had asked me to go to New York to work on costumes and be her personal manager; we made tentative plans for me to go there at Christmas.

During that summer in Santa Barbara I went to the mission for Mass and some of their Bible studies, knowing that I needed to keep strong in the Word and be with other believers. But when I wasn't around other Christians I was in the world of the stage and performing. As wonderful as the people were, their lifestyles were some of the most ungodly I had ever seen.

The thrill of the stage, the opera, the music, and the drama enveloped me. I wholeheartedly threw myself into whatever was needed, and it wasn't long before my Christianity took a back seat to the theatre, with all the worldliness and excitement that the theatre holds surrounding most of my waking hours.

At the end of the summer I was very thankful for the experience and the teaching, but I was more thankful to be back in Canada and my little place. I had a full load of teaching that fall, going to Victoria every Monday, teaching university students who were taking singing as a second major. It was a new level of teaching for me, and I quite enjoyed the challenge.

By now Bob had been gone over a year and half, and still every couple weeks I would phone Shirley and ask if she had heard from him. The answer was always the same; she hadn't. For some reason I knew in my heart that he would be back. It was just a feeling, but it was a very strong one.

As the weeks passed, I made the decision to not go to New York at Christmas. Back home and in my regular, less glamorous routine, I realized that the singer I would be personal manager to was very controlling, and I feared getting into a situation where I had none of my own control again. I quite happily made the decision to turn down her offer.

It was the end of September 1974, and I was not feeling well. I stayed home from work and called my old neighbour just to chat. As we were about to hang up, I commented that all I needed now was for Bob to show up.

I hung up the phone, and it immediately began to ring.

"Hello, Grace?"

I knew that voice and could not believe I was hearing it.

"Bob?"

A Real Marriage

Love never fails
[never fades out or becomes obsolete or comes to an end].
1 Corinthians 13:8

It had been eighteen months since Bob walked out of my life. I thought of him often, although as the months went by I never really asked myself how I felt about him. At first there was so much disbelief, hurt, uncertainty, and anger that I just allowed those emotions to carry me. True to form, I hadn't really dealt with any of them, so when I heard his voice that day, my heart skipped a beat.

Just like old times, we began to talk. Or, rather, he began to talk and I listened. He told me that he was currently in the interior of British Columbia, in Vernon (approximately 600 kilometres from Victoria). After he left me he found a job on a freighter and eventually landed in England. There he went to see his mother, whom he had not seen in over twenty years, and mended the relationship. Now he wanted to mend the relationship with me and asked if I would be willing to meet with him.

He also told me that he had worked on his relationship with the Lord and was back walking with him. That was probably the only thing he could have said that would make me even think about meeting him again. Even though my own faith was a little bit shaky after the summer in California, and at times I ignored it completely, I knew that the only way we could even connect as friends would be if we shared the faith that we had found together.

As our conversation continued, my mind whirled. I couldn't just forget what he had done to me, the lies he had told. On the other hand, what's done is done, I thought, and what he had done in the past was exactly that, the past. It was not mine to carry around or to deal with. Bob seemed genuinely remorseful and eager to see me.

He explained that he had met a woman in Manitoba and was getting serious about her, but he inadvertently kept calling her Grace. After several incidents like this, she suggested that Bob go back to me to see if our story was in actuality over. And that was what he was doing.

After all the stories he asked me again if I would meet him. I didn't stop to allow my mind to enter the decision-making process. When my heart told my mouth to say yes, that is exactly what I did. I agreed to meet him.

He suggested that we meet at a gas station about halfway between our cities, and I immediately knew which gas station he meant. I had never been there before, there was no significance whatsoever to it, but I seemed to know intuitively which one it was.

I hung up the phone, and the emotions began. I was excited to see Bob again, which made me wonder if I still loved him. I was also nervous, scared, and little bit angry. Nonetheless, I didn't have time to dwell on it. Or perhaps I chose not to take the time to dwell on it.

I talked to Shirley, and she cautioned me, reminding me of who Bob had shown himself to be in the past. But I figured I would just go and see what would come of it all. So I cancelled all my lessons, bought a new suitcase, and left to meet the most exciting man I had ever known, choosing not to think of all the betrayal and hurt.

There was something about Bob that was just plain exciting. If someone had asked me the week before if I would consider driving 300 kilometres to meet Bob after eighteen months of silence, I might have laughed and said, "Of course not!" But hearing his voice and talking to him again just drew me in, and I simply could not stay away.

I arrived early in the evening and drove straight to the gas station. There was Bob, waiting for me, and did he ever look good to me! He seemed to have an air of confidence around him that he hadn't had when we were together, and he was genuinely happy to see me. He gave me a real kiss, something that had been seriously lacking in our relationship previously, and I was hooked!

We went out for coffee together, and it was so comfortable to be with him again. He told me he was painting again and going to church again. He really seemed to have gotten his life back in order.

We decided that I would leave my car at the gas station and travel together to Vernon in his. We arrived at his place quite late, but when I lay down on my bed I couldn't fall asleep; there was too much to think about, too much to sort through.

The next afternoon Bob asked me to marry him.

Just like that. That easily, that quickly.

I didn't think of saying no to him, but I did know that there would have to be conditions. I told him that this time I would need a real marriage, one before God in a church. I also wanted a strong and healthy sex life. Previously we had lived together more like brother and sister, and I didn't want to be married like that. I also demanded that there would be no more unfaithfulness; I needed to know that I could trust him. I didn't think these things would be all that difficult if he truly was walking with the Lord.

Bob agreed to everything that I asked of him, wanting the same things from our relationship that I did.

And so we started to make plans. On Sunday we went to church together, and I met his friends. In the afternoon he showed me the paintings he had been working on. He was shy and afraid to ask my opinion, but there was no hesitation on my part in telling him that they were beautiful, possibly the best he had ever done. He was visibly relieved and told me that he was planning a show in Vernon and would really like it if I was there with him.

We spent all our time together that weekend getting to know each other in a way that I felt was for real this time. I sensed a change in him, and I wasn't afraid at all to let the past go and look toward the future. Hours passed as he showed me different places he liked to go, mountains he enjoyed spending time on. He was concerned about his mother and how she was getting involved in some sort of spiritualism that he knew was opposite to our Christianity, and we talked about bringing her over to Canada to live with us.

Before I left to go back home we set our wedding date for December 21, less than three months away.

Back home I excitedly shared my news with Shirley and all my friends. I was confident that it would all work this time because Christ would be the head of our home. What could go wrong under him?

I continued to teach for those few months but told my students I wouldn't be back after the Christmas break. I sold my business (my good name and my students) and prepared to get married and move away. The wedding would be on the island, but then we would set up home in Vernon. Shirley was my bridesmaid, and I sewed my own dress out of a deep green velvet fabric.

The wedding was lovely and was followed by a reception at Shirley and Graham's. I was absolutely thrilled with the way everything went and was convinced all would be well now.

After the reception Bob and I drove to our hotel, where I got ready for bed and waited for him. When he finally came to bed he was very disturbed. He finally told me that he wanted to consummate our marriage but just couldn't.

I should have known then that things were not right, but I really believed that with the Lord's help everything would work out.

I got out of bed and got dressed. We went for a walk on the breakwater together before turning in for the night.

The next morning we consummated our marriage and continued on as if our wedding night had never happened.

Journeying into the Unknown

When a man's ways please the Lord, He makes even his enemies to
be at peace with him.
Proverbs 16:7

I knew Bob loved me; there was never a doubt in my mind of that. I also knew that on the surface our marriage looked great. However, if you could look underneath you would see all the hurt accumulated over the decades individually, as well as the years of hurt that we had caused together but never resolved. We never talked about problems; we just kept moving forward, teaching, painting, singing, playing piano, performing and doing shows, both theatrical and with Bob's art.

Bob was always the one on centre stage, even when there were no performances. He was very involved in what I did, to the point of taking over. When I opened the concert series, Bob had to be the emcee. When we were working on a production, things were done Bob's way, including him picking out the design and fabrics for my clothing. Only in the area of music would I have any say, and that only because I had more expertise than he had.

We had begun to make arrangements for Bob's mother to come over from England and live with us. With this in mind, we bought a two-storey house with three bedrooms. It was a bit of a fixer-upper, but neither of us shied away from hard work. We were thrilled to find hardwood flooring under the wall-to-wall green shag carpet in the living room but dismayed when we took down a wall to enlarge the living room and found very old parallel wiring.

The bedroom that we chose for Mum was on the second floor, under the eaves. It reminded me a little of my childhood home in Saskatchewan, and I took extra care to make it pretty. We painted the room a lovely blue and put in a canopy bed with a matching easy chair. When all was said and done, it was a room that I was enchanted with. So when Mum came to live with us and told me she hated the colour blue, preferring pink, I was hurt. Nonetheless, I made every effort to welcome her and do things to please her.

It quickly became apparent that nothing I did pleased her. For one thing, I continued to call Bob by the only name I had ever known him as, Bob. She, of course, only knew her son by the name she had given him and so insisted on calling him that, making it very clear that I should too.

They say that it is very difficult for women to please their mother-in-laws, that mothers feel very protective of their sons. Whether or not that was the case with Bob's mom, I don't know, but we never hit it off. I tried to love her, but it soon became obvious that the two of us could not live under the same roof.

Every time we all went to visit Shirley and Graham, Mum would comment on the beauty of their house and how much she enjoyed Shirley's company. Before long, someone suggested that she move in with them, and I have to say it was a relief when she made that move. With Shirley and Graham she felt like the queen mum, and it certainly made for an easier life for us.

Bob and I went to several churches while living in Vernon and started hearing a familiar teaching throughout them about the end times. Over and over we heard messages about Christ's return and the tribulation that might come before the final destruction. During that tribulation, we were told, things would get very difficult for Christians. Great persecution was in store. There would be the mark of the beast, without which you could not hold down a job, make purchases, own property, etc. And, most importantly, it didn't look like it would be long before it all happened.

Like many others in the seventies, Bob and I looked around us and agreed we were heading towards the end times. When Bob suggested that we start thinking about having a place that was completely self-contained, where we could live independently and not need anything the world would demand of us, I did what I did best. I agreed. I never stopped to think that we should just stay put and trust the Lord. I put my trust in my husband instead.

This wasn't the first time that we had wanted to get away from everything, that running away appealed to us. It was a little different than sailing to a deserted island, but only marginally. The idea of living all on our own seemed to never have left us, and this doctrine of suffering through tribulation worked quite well with who Bob and I were.

Bob had held several shows and done a series of sketches that had sold very well. I was teaching forty hours a week, and so between us we were able to meet all our bills. We had very little in the way of savings, but we felt confident that we could sell our home and with that money buy a place in the middle of nowhere.

We began to look for property, excited to be on the edge of an adventure again. We drove to various places in the remote areas of British Columbia. One property up north looked very appealing, with its own small lake and potential for a Christmas tree business. We made an offer, subject to the sale of our own house. Unfortunately the owner had another offer before our home sold, and we had no choice but to let it go. I was very sorry that the deal fell through but very confident that the Lord had other plans.

And so we kept looking. Every summer we would venture to a different part of British Columbia, not wanting to rule out any rural areas, patiently believing that when we found the perfect place for us we would know.

During this time of searching for property, Bob had a short-term job in Vancouver and was away for a week. One evening I tried to call him and just couldn't connect with him. No matter when I called, he just wasn't there. It didn't take long for the fear to set in that he had taken off again or had fallen in with some of his old buddies who I knew were bad news for him. Once those thoughts entered my head, they swirled over and over, each scenario presenting itself worse than the last.

Repeatedly phoning him, long past the time he should have been back in his room, I was inconsolable, and the tears were streaming down my face. Finally deciding to go to bed, I was washing my face when I heard the Lord speak to me.

"Take your hands off him."

I heard his voice as clear as if he were standing there beside me as a man. Even today I can hear those five words. "Take your hands off him."

My tears dried up and I answered him.

"Okay, Lord, he is in your hands."

Right then I gave Bob over to him, right into his hands, hands that were bigger and so much more capable than mine to care for him. I wish I could say it was a one-time gift, but over the months and years to come, I repeatedly took Bob back into my hands before I was reminded to relinquish him.

Another thing happened during that week alone. I was praying by my bedside one evening, talking to God about him being my Father, which I found very hard to think of. With the earthly example that I had, I simply could not fathom what it meant. Seeing him as my Father was more negative than positive, and yet everything I read in the Bible spoke of a loving figure. I struggled with that whole concept and so I brought it to him to figure out.

While in prayer, I was suddenly flooded with God's love, as if I was being showered with all the love I would ever need. There was no explanation except that God heard my prayer and wanted to show me that he *was* my Father and he loved me beyond anything I had ever known. I knew then that God was indeed my loving heavenly Father and what it felt like to be loved.

It was an experience that I have never forgotten and have often thanked him for. It was that love that would keep me going in the difficult times that were yet to come.

Moving to a Remote and Isolated Location

Come to Me, all you who labor and are heavy-laden and
overburdened, and I will cause you to rest.
[I will ease and relieve and refresh your souls.]
Matthew 11:28

We kept our eyes open for some wilderness property, and while on a trip for Bob's work we found what we were looking for. His mom was with us, and when we got to Prince Rupert it was raining so heavily that we turned around and headed to Burns Lake. We were hoping to find a motel there, but they were all full, so we headed a few more miles south.

We found another small lake and rented a wonderful rustic cabin with a woodstove. It was cozy and absolutely perfect. We fell in love with the area, and the next day we asked around about property for sale.

In the real estate office we found out about a forty-four-acre piece of land on the south side of Francois Lake. It had a lot of standing timber on it, which we could sell to bring in a great deal of money. We expressed our interest to the agent, but he didn't offer to show us the place, so Bob and I drove out on our own.

Francois Lake is in the centre of British Columbia, thirty kilometres south of Burns Lake. It is a large lake and very beautiful. The property that we were interested in had no road access, so that first day we simply drove to the area and looked around. We were so excited by what we saw that the next morning we took Mum with us and rented a boat to go over and see the actual property.

We were excited to find that there was an old cabin on the land, even though the roof of it had fallen in. The closest neighbour on the lake was about a mile away. When the wind started blowing in the afternoon, we were forced to meet the neighbours, as Mum was afraid to go back over in the little boat we had rented. The neighbours had a bigger boat and very kindly and happily took Mum and I over to the mainland again while Bob went back in the rented boat. They seemed very pleased at the thought of us buying the property, and we were just as pleased to meet such fine people and possibly consider them as neighbours.

We didn't make an offer right then; instead we decided to talk to our realtor in Vernon. Our trip back home was filled with excitement as we talked about the future and realizing our dreams for solitude and living off the land using our own hands. I was very much drawn to the simple life of a pioneer, getting back to the land. Much of my life had been simple, from working hard on the farm to the life in the convent, so following Bob with this dream was not a hardship for me at all.

It wasn't long before we began putting our thoughts into actions, making preparations to move. We bought the new place and listed our house. As time went on and it didn't sell, we decided to just give it back to the bank. We were eager to get going on our adventure now that we had found the perfect property; we had waited long enough, and nothing was going to hold us back. Our friends back home supported our move with gifts such as a shotgun, a small rifle, and a whole roll of chain for our chainsaw, and by July 1979 we were ready to make our big move.

We arrived at Francois Lake with a huge pile of belongings, and we began to ferry things across the lake with a small boat and outboard motor. This was no easy task, and we knew it would take quite some time. Yet before we knew it, neighbours arrived with their big river boats and began helping us. We were astounded that that kind of neighbourly kindness was still in existence, and it confirmed our decision to live there.

Once on our property we began to set up our three-man tent that we planned to live in while we worked on making the cabin habitable. Our new friends wouldn't hear of it. They brought out a wall tent and proceeded to put it up. The tent, made out of heavy canvas, had four straight walls, was at least ten feet across, and felt more like a small house. It was so much more pleasant than a tiny tent, and we could keep our personal belongings in there with us.

I made a temporary kitchen out of an old shed facing the yard that still had one wall standing. I added a shelf and covered it with some heavy plastic washable table coverings, and there was my kitchen! I couldn't have wanted anything more right then.

I had a fire pit that I cooked over and even learned to make bread over the open fire. I put a brick in a large pot and my bread pan on top of that. With the cover on the pot, I could make a great loaf of bread and excellent biscuits. Cakes were not quite as simple, but we enjoyed whatever came out of my "oven."

Tackling the cabin was a little daunting. We first had to clean it in order to see what work was needed. That involved shovelling out the four-foot pile of pack rat items and leaves that covered the floor. But we were not afraid of hard work and willingly started shovelling. We came up with our own little system. One of us would shovel the debris into the wheelbarrow and the other would haul it down the trail and throw it all over a bank.

It took us several days to clear out the cabin and see the floor. Then we could take a good look at the walls, and we discovered that the cabin was well-built. The builder had squared the logs with an axe and interlocked the log ends, then put boards upright on the inside and filled the space between the logs and the boards with old underwear. Needless to say, the pack rats had a great time in there.

We began pulling all those boards off, a nasty job that left us covered with flying debris. I had never been so dirty before, not even on the farm growing up. Several times a day we felt it necessary to take a break and go wash in the lake.

Once we had the walls clear, we turned our attention back to the floor and began taking up the rotten plywood. We were astonished to

125

find that under those rotting boards there was a beautiful, clean plywood floor. In the midst of all the dirt, grime, and rubbish we were immersed in, this was such a treat.

When Bob began working on replacing the roof, one of our neighbours came over with a boatload of lumber from his saw mill. So we cut new logs for rafters and hoisted them up. The hardest was the peak log. We used a block and tackle, and Bob went up to secure it. I had a hard time watching him climb around on bare logs; he could have slipped so easily.

Once the rafters and the peak log were on, three of the neighbouring men helped us sheet the roof and cover those boards with several layers of heavy tarpaper.

Finally we came to the point where we were able to make a door and close our little house up.

I began chinking the log walls, and when that was done I painted them all white. What a difference that made, and how rewarding all the work was!

The back room was both our bedroom and a storage room for all the canning I had done in preparation for the winter, so we built a series of shelves to hold it all. I hung some old heavy curtains in front of the shelves, just to look a little nicer. We built a high bed, in order to store our belongings underneath it, put our camping foam on top of it, and moved in.

It was an exciting day when we moved everything from our wall tent into our house. The kitchen stove was hooked up to the chimney, and it was surprisingly smoke-free. Above it hung a food dryer. A wooden box held our washbasin. An old table had been left in the cabin and needed only a plastic cloth to make it functional. Curtains from past kitchens needed only minor adjustments before I could hang them. We had two easy chairs with us, including the one we had bought for Bob's mom's bedroom, and behind each of our chairs we had gaslights on the wall. A gas chandelier gave light to the table. Bob had traded one of his paintings for a bear rug, and it hung over the door to our bedroom.

We had found some linoleum ends, and these fit quite nicely in our kitchen–living area. With the braided rug from my former studio, the room was quaint and cozy, and one that we considered quite perfect for us.

A small generator ran the water pump, but we only pumped water up to the house when we needed a lot for bathing or washing clothes. We could boat across the lake to a resort and do our laundry there, but I preferred to do it at home in our wooden washing machine that we had found in Saskatchewan. With the wringer on it, it made washday much easier than if I had to do it all by hand. I wasn't complaining; my farm upbringing came in very handy.

Life was simple for us at Francois Lake. Bob would get up and light the fire in the kitchen stove first thing in the morning, and that was enough to warm the house most days. Then we would have breakfast and our time of devotions together. While I cleaned up after our meal, Bob would check outside to make sure all was well. Then he would settle in to the day's work, and I would sew, bake, and do laundry or housework.

Some heavy work needed to be done, like bringing in our wood for the winter, and we did it together. There was a lot of deadfall very close by, and we would drag the logs in with a yoke between us. When the neighbours heard what we were doing, they got together. One Saturday they walked a skidder across our bay shore and proceeded to drag in enough trees to last a few years. They wouldn't take anything for their work except a pie, which I was more than happy to give them.

We were loving the life that we had created and feeling contented with the choice we had made to move. We were completely settled in when winter came, and we experienced the beauty of a true Canadian winter. The days were cold, the nights colder, but we had all we needed. The lake froze over, and you could often see people taking advantage of the lazier winter days by skating on the lake or ice fishing.

We were able to finance the small things that we needed through the gallery that Bob was commissioned by, and so it was a huge blow when we discovered that the gallery had gone bankrupt. By the time early spring rolled around, we realized that income was going to be a problem.

Left with no choice, Bob went out to see what he could do, and I stayed in our cabin to keep the fires stoked so that our supplies wouldn't freeze. I enjoyed the rare solitude. We had a two-way radio that we used to keep in touch with the neighbours, so I wasn't completely on my own. I made sure before it got dark that I had enough wood for the night, and I was as secure as could be.

On the night that I expected Bob back I was busy in the house when suddenly he walked in and said, "Didn't you hear the horn?" I couldn't imagine what he was talking about. I followed him outside, where I saw a Jeep. He had traded our old van for it and driven it across the ice to our place!

I was so excited to have him home again! That afternoon I had seen the most beautiful fisher, a member of the weasel family, with a tail about three feet long. I was hoping that it would show up again so that Bob could see it.

But it was not to be. Bob informed me that he had done all that he could, but there was no income coming in. We would both have to leave our little property. While that was sad, I saw it as a temporary measure, and we were both determined that we would come back. In the meantime, we packed up what we could, gave some things to the neighbours, and off we went. We hadn't even spent an entire year there when we found ourselves crossing the lake to leave it.

The drive back across the lake was hair-raising. By now the melting process had started, and every time we hit a crack in the ice, the water would splash up over us. I was convinced we were going down. I was relieved when we finally made it safely across and were on solid ground again.

We were headed back to Vernon when the Jeep began leaking oil. We stopped, added oil, and drove on. Before long the oil light would come on again, and we'd have to stop again and add more oil. We knew there was a problem, but we hoped to get home before getting it checked out.

About four hours from our destination, we ran out of oil. The Jeep finally came to a stop about one mile outside of a little town called Blue River. Bob walked into town while I stayed in the vehicle. I was praying earnestly that someone would stop and pick him up when the Lord spoke to me again. This time it was not audible but in a word picture.

I saw a clear picture of a child who was always carried, and his backbone was never able to grow strong. I knew instantly that this was what I was doing. I was carrying Bob with my own faith instead of letting him develop his own.

The next few days convinced me that he needed to have his own faith.

The Last of Bob

Roll your works upon the Lord [commit and trust them wholly to Him; He will cause your thoughts to become agreeable to His will, and] so shall your plans be established and succeed.
Proverbs 16:3

Fixing the Jeep was not a simple matter. We stayed in a motel that night, and the next day we had to have the Jeep towed all the way to Vernon. Back home it was discovered that the motor was irreparable, and so we were left without a vehicle.

We also did not have a place to live so called upon some old friends, Jack and June. They graciously took us in, even though we had no idea how long we would need accommodations.

At this point we had no jobs, no place to live, and now no vehicle. It ended up being almost a month before we were able to move on.

We managed to trade in our broken-down Jeep for an older car, and it drove very well. Bob began to look for work while I stayed with June. She was a wonderful Christian lady whom I had known for many years. To pay our way, I painted her living room and did some sewing for her. While our stay was an imposition on her and Jack, it was a blessing to be there. We spent much of our time talking about the Lord, and we prayed together.

When Bob couldn't find any work in town he went up to Edmonton, Alberta, to look. He came back home to say that Edmonton was a booming city and we were both quite likely to find work. So at the end of April 1980 we moved again.

We immediately began looking for a place to rent, preferably in the country. Rather aimlessly we started driving through the rural parts of Edmonton. After some time we came to a farm that had a Scripture verse on a sign in the yard. We drove in and asked the owners if they knew of anyone who might have a house to rent in the country.

As it turned out, a neighbour across the field had an empty house for rent. They phoned over, and we were invited to take a look.

We drove onto the property and saw a beautiful tidy yard with flowers and trees. The owners, Cyril and Margaret, were not sure they wanted to rent it out just yet. Cyril's mother had lived there until she passed away the previous fall, and they hadn't decided yet what to do with the vacant home.

We chatted for a while, and at the end of our conversation they told us that we were welcome to rent the house. That was the very best thing to happen to us; Cyril and Margaret became very close friends and would be invaluable to me as support in the coming months and years.

The very next morning we moved into our new home. The house was built in the 1940s and had two bedrooms, one of them housing a sewing machine that I was free to use. The kitchen was bright and cheery; the living room, with a mock fireplace, was warm and cozy. The entire house was furnished, right down to dishes and linens. We did not take this gift from the Lord lightly.

The next day was a Saturday, and in the morning Cyril came rushing to our door to announce that the church they were in the process of building was on fire. Bob immediately went with him to the site to see what could be done. He was gone all day and came home covered with soot. Through his ashes and grime he told me that he had volunteered me to sing at their service the following day.

God certainly had his hand on our lives. The school that the church was meeting in while their new building was being built was scheduled to open in September, and they agreed to allow me to teach music there.

Cyril's daughter, who worked in an office building on the way into Edmonton, told Bob about some rooms available that he could use for a studio, and so he immediately went to get his art supplies.

The summer was filled with anticipation for us. Bob was busy painting again and finding work. I was doing some work around the house and painting for Cyril and Margaret. We made several trips back to Francois Lake as we shared our vision for the property with couples we met at church.

But while I thought things were moving forward and was excited to see where the Lord would lead us, Bob began to drift away from me. We had been married for five years, and for the first time in our marriage he seemed to be distant from me.

One evening he came home extremely late, in the wee hours of the morning, and as soon as he walked in I knew that he had been with someone. I could smell an unfamiliar fragrance on him. Without a word, he went to the bathroom and vomited before coming to bed, very contrite.

Whoever he was with, whatever he had done that night, caused him great anguish. Even though he was sorry and told me so, things were not good for him. He went to talk to the one of the pastors of our church, but it did not seem to help him.

It became apparent that he wanted to run. He started worrying about the debts we had, and he just wanted to get out. Together we went to talk to two couples who were good friends, and the men had a good long chat with Bob. For a few days he seemed to be better.

He decided to take a trip to the Rocky Mountains to gather material for his work. His mother was visiting us at the time, and as he had spent some time with her already he felt it was okay to leave. He would be taking the car, but I knew I would be okay without it as long as he was back by the weekend.

He left on a Monday morning at 9 a.m., and by 10 a.m. I knew he had left me.

I looked in Bob's dresser drawers and saw that his passport was gone. I could not say a thing to his mother. There were no words, and I didn't have the heart.

A little later there was a phone call from a client of his who had scheduled a meeting with him that morning. On the outside I had to act as if all was well, while inside the tears were streaming. I had no one to talk to as Cyril and Margaret had gone away for a few days, so I kept everything inside me.

For three days I pretended all was well, and on Thursday Cyril's daughter drove Bob's mom and me to the airport. I watched as Mum boarded her plane to go back home, not having any idea that her son had run away from his life once again.

After she was gone I felt free to go to Bob's studio and see how he left things. What I saw confirmed what I already knew. His good works were gone, as well as all his supplies. He had very obviously planned his leaving and was gone for good.

I had no money, no car, nothing. I worked around the house on the Friday, and on Saturday Cyril and Margaret came home. I poured out all that had happened that week. As the tears coursed down my face, I was thankful for these two dear friends who were there to guide me through the nightmare I found myself in.

Ever practical, Margaret drove me to the mailbox, and there I found a letter from Bob. He told me he had to find himself and that he still loved me. He asked me to wait for him.

Cyril and Margaret had a difficult time trying to understand what Bob had done. They thought they knew him, but of course they knew only what Bob wanted them to know. I think I was the only person to ever even partially understand him. I could understand the force that drove him. Of course I didn't approve of his choices or ways of dealing with his pain, but I believed that I understood a small part of what he was going through.

That evening I had a phone call from Shirley and Graham. They had felt that there was a need in my life and had come to be with me. Shirley and I often sensed when the other of us had a need. It was so good to see them and share with them what had been going on. They settled in to help me wherever needed.

I couldn't stop the clock and calendar while I adjusted and learned to cope. September was fast approaching, and I would be expected at the school to begin music lessons for the students. I was struck with the impracticality of my situation. When we moved to Francois Lake I gave away all my clothing that wasn't suited to wilderness living, leaving me with no suitable clothing to teach in.

Again I found myself grateful for a practical presence as Graham gave me $200 and Shirley directed me to Western Wool Mills, which was closing its doors and having a huge sale. Together we bought all the fabric I would need to make a new wardrobe.

From there the three of us headed to Bob's studio. We once again dug in to clean up Bob's things, storing it all in Cyril's barn. They also took me grocery shopping. It's astounding to me how the details of living can be forgotten or pushed aside during a traumatic experience. Shirley and Graham helped me refocus on putting one foot in front of the other in the practical details. They were there when I had to contact all the people who had commissioned work from Bob and tell them he would be unable to complete their contracts.

During that time I inadvertently met the man Bob had been with the night he came home ill at three in the morning. His cologne set him apart and made me realize it was him. I asked if he knew where Bob went, but he had no idea. It was strange to talk to him, and I was again glad that Shirley was with me.

Shirley and Graham stayed with me for a little over one week, and I don't know how I would have managed without them. I treasured their friendship, their faith, and their strength.

With no other choice, I began to get ready to teach, taking calls for new students and finishing up my wardrobe. Knowing that I was not equipped to deal with all that had happened, I began counselling with a pastor at church.

I gathered all the information about the money Bob and I owed, and it came to quite a large sum. I didn't know what I was going to do. When I shared that information with Cyril, he gave me a month's free rent and an introduction to his lawyer.

The lawyer contacted all the people that we were indebted to and offered so much on each dollar owed. All but one accepted the offer. The one who didn't demanded to be paid in full.

I didn't know what to do. I couldn't ask Cyril and Margaret for a loan as they had already done so much for me. The thought came to me that the father of one of my students was in a position that he could loan me the money. Without wanting to presume anything, I first asked my counsellor what he thought about it. He agreed that it was a good idea.

The next time I saw this dad I blurted out my request in the middle of a hallway. He didn't even hesitate before he said, "Of course."

I couldn't believe my ears. At the very least I would have expected him to ask for some sort of collateral, but all he wanted was my word.

I began the process of paying off all the creditors that Bob and I owed and then began making payments to my benefactor.

As time went on, I gradually relearned how to make decisions on my own. More and more students were coming my way, and I found all sorts of different jobs that used my talents. For a while I did some catering, as well as some piecework for a wool shop in Edmonton. Very slowly I was paying back my debts and making ends meet. While the pain of Bob's desertion didn't leave me, keeping very busy was a good thing for my mind.

This time around being on my own was very different than the first time Bob left. This time I was grounded in the Lord and knew how to trust him with the details of my life. There was no doubt in my mind that I could do nothing without him, and so life in some ways was actually easier.

Every morning I would get up early enough to spend a half hour with God, reading Scripture, praying, or just spending time in his presence. Yet there were times where I wasn't all that happy with him.

One morning I asked God why all of this had happened to me. He wasn't giving me an answer as quickly as I wanted, and I became impatient. I stomped around getting ready for work, constantly nagging him for an answer but not getting one. By the time I left for work I felt that God had let me down. I deserved an answer!

As I was driving, I screamed at him as loud as I could. I expected to feel so much better for letting off steam. Instead I felt a bit of shame, even though there was no doubt that God was okay with my outburst.

I did a lot of singing at church, and at times that I could feel God's presence as real as the air around me, a burning heaviness that enveloped me. One Good Friday morning I sang "Behold the Man" by Jimmy Owens. God's love so overwhelmed me that by the end of the song I was in tears. I sat back down for communion, and the tears kept flowing. It was a service that has stayed close in my memory all these years.

It was because of the Lord that I was able to face some things about Bob, what our marriage really was. And the beauty of it all was that Jesus was replacing Bob with himself. He became my strength, my companion, my shield.

Of course I was nowhere near perfect and never will be. I had many stumbles and falls as I tried to make my way through this time with the Lord instead of without him, like I'd done so often in the past. The difference was that no matter how many times I stumbled, how many falls I took, I knew that Jesus would forgive me each time I came to him and confessed my failings.

God helped me find who I really am. All my life I had allowed others to take control of me, make my decisions. Now as I spent time with God he gave me the strength to see the things that needed changing in me, as well as showing me what I could do when I was in him. Very slowly he gave me confidence to be the person he made me to be. Jesus was finally becoming first in my life, and nothing was going to change that.

I felt very fortunate to still be living in the rented farmhouse, because Cyril and Margaret were constant examples to me of what a real Christian marriage was. They were always there for me, continuously lifting me up to the Lord in prayer.

Just before Christmas I received a note from Bob. He was in the Bahamas, he still loved me, but he had to find himself.

Complete Healing and Restoration

He will feed His flock like a shepherd: He will gather the lambs
in His arm, He will carry them in his bosom and will gently lead
those that have their young.
Isaiah 40:11

It was the third spring after Bob had left. Teaching was going relatively well, and I was enjoying my students and the school. During the three years we had presented two musicals, which were challenging but very successful.

Healing was slow. I had been hanging on to the possibility that Bob might still come back to me. One morning I was in a counselling session when my counsellor advised me to pursue a divorce.

I began talking about it and suddenly burst into tears. It had finally dawned on me that my marriage was really and truly over. For the first time I admitted that it had not been a real marriage after about the second year.

As I sat in that counsellor's office, I poured out how Bob was always very affectionate and loving, but he very seldom kissed me and we rarely had sex. As the words flowed, I realized the obvious for the first time. Bob had homosexual tendencies.

My counsellor told me that he had known this for some time, but it was something I needed to realize on my own. Even after meeting the man Bob had been with the night he came home so late, I never really allowed the thought that he was gay to enter my head.

Now it entered and stayed. Admitting the truth freed me to really let go of our marriage, file for divorce, and move forward. After two years without a word from Bob, I finally was able to give his clothes away and get rid of his old shoes that were still by the back door.

I was feeling the stress of all this. After I hit a student across the hand with a pencil, I realized that I needed a change. That was so out of character for me that I knew I needed to step back from teaching for a while.

I informed the principal that this would be my last year and that I would be looking for some other employment. It wasn't long before he called me into his office, having just heard of a summer job at a Christian camp. They were looking for a cook, and after an interview I prepared myself for another journey.

I would continue to teach five of my students in my home, but other than them my life became all about camp and cooking. At the end of the summer I would have loved to stay on, but the pay was not enough for me to continue paying off my debts, so in September I was out of work.

One day I was in the Edmonton Savings and Credit Union and offhandedly asked about any available jobs. I was directed to the manager. Sitting in her office I began to tell her my story. She asked a few questions and then said to me, "You don't recognize me, do you?"

I looked at her more closely but had to admit that, no, I didn't. She then informed me that I had taught her music while I was in the convent, and she had played the role of the witch in our musical, *Hansel and Gretel*. We both had a good laugh at how small the world really is.

As far as a job went, there was an opening in another branch, and she put in a good word for me. So I found myself being a teller and a receptionist. God never ceased to amaze me with how he took care of me.

In the meantime I proceeded with the divorce and was getting ready for the court hearing that I had to attend. Three days before I was to appear, I had a phone call from a friend in Vernon. She had just read a story in a major newspaper about Bob trying to raise funds to sail around the world to advertise for the World Expo that was scheduled to take place in Vancouver a few years from then.

This was the first I had heard of him in three years, and I wasn't sure how the knowledge of his whereabouts would affect the hearing. I called my lawyer, who in turn spoke to the judge. At my hearing, I was granted a divorce. The only change was that if Bob ever came into money I would be entitled to spousal support.

Meanwhile I wasn't sure what to do about Bob. Should I call him? Let him know that he was a free man? Perhaps I should just leave well enough alone.

I talked to friends, who all thought if I did call him I should not be alone. I prayed about it, and one evening it just felt right to phone him. And so I did.

It was strange to hear his voice again. He sounded almost numb and very distant. I let him know about the divorce and that I wasn't angry with him, that in some ways I understood why he left.

He told me that he had written to me in the last year, but I hadn't received any letters, so I'm not sure if that was just another one of the lies that he was so used to telling. After a few minutes, there seemed to be nothing left to say, so I hung up the phone. As calm as I had felt during the call, I now sat there shaking.

There was one last phone call from Bob. He was in the Maritimes and wanted to get married again but discovered that our divorce was not final. That was a mere technicality, needing only a few hundred dollars to finalize.

Several years later I heard that he was in the Victoria area again, remarried. I also learned that he was still running. The last word I ever heard about him was a rumour that he had been murdered, but that has never been confirmed.

The chapter in my life called "Bob" was firmly and completely over.

Another was about to begin.

Lord of My Life

Sing to Him a new song; play skillfully [on the strings] with a loud and joyful sound. For the word of the Lord is right; and all His work is done in faithfulness.
Psalm 33:3-4

A new Grace had emerged in the four years since Bob walked away for the second and last time. The last dream shattered, his walking out, was not the worst by far, and that was only because I now had God to help me get through. My relationship with him continued to grow.

My life felt like it was on somewhat of an even keel, working at the credit union, very involved with music at church, and supporting myself. I was doing a little bit of teaching still, and almost all my bills were paid. I was beginning to plan for the future.

Yet there still seemed to be something not quite right. Things were not settled within me, and I started to feel like I wasn't able to function quite as well. I had no idea what it was and even less as to what to do about it. I am forever thankful that God works with us, no matter where we are in our lives, sometimes just stepping in to take care of what we need.

For me it happened during a week of meetings at church. One evening I was sitting in the pew listening to the speaker. His message was on the authority of God. I heard him say that we have to give everything to God. "Each morning you have to place yourself under the authority and protection of God," he said. And a light bulb went off in my head.

Yes, I had accepted Christ, but had I really made him Lord of my life? It was all about the Kingship of Christ, giving him the proper place in my life.

I began to give every part of my life over to the Lord. I looked at every dream I had ever had that had shattered. I knew I had to take each one and properly hand it over to the one who would know what to do with it.

My very first dream of having a relationship with him, while shattered for a while and now beautifully restored, was still one I needed to give over to him. I laid down the dream to have friendships in the convent. I thought of my dream to have a career on stage and humbly put it at his feet. The dream I mourned over the longest, that of a home, a husband, and children, I gently laid in his arms. The dream of sailing to a deserted island had to be relinquished, and the dream of being married to Bob had to be let go of and laid at his throne. The dream of Francoise Lake and the simple life was the toughest one to open my hands to let loose because I still owned it. Yet in order to make Christ Lord of everything, eventually I surrendered that, too.

I had finally brought my dreams to the right person, and when I knew he was Lord of my life, my life settled down. Every morning of every day I spent the first thirty minutes with him, giving him everything.

God was in charge. There were no other dreams to follow. I had finally got to the end of myself and lived my life according to Christ, not me. No one was going to change the new Grace that God had made. She was rooted and strong in Christ.

It was February 1984. My counsellor had moved to Montreal to pastor a large church and called me to offer me the position of music minister. I was very interested and decided that I would go there in April to meet everyone and see how I fit in with the congregation. I was very excited about this new ministry, and life felt complete.

But God had a different plan in mind.

I kept running into a couple at church, and every time we met they told me that I simply had to meet their brother, Ivan. At the beginning of

March they invited me to Sunday dinner after church. Ivan was in town, and they wanted us to meet. The whole idea of dating and marriage made me laugh, but I was excited enough to care about what to wear.

That lunch was like no other I had ever experienced. Another couple was there as well, so that made six of us, which made for an easy flow of conversation. Every time I tried to sneak a glance at Ivan, he was sneaking a glance at me.

After lunch, we all were led into the living room, but within a few minutes everyone else had disappeared, leaving Ivan and me alone. We began talking, and four hours later we were still talking. We never seemed to run out of things to say and, in fact, had many things in common. He loved to fish and camp, and when I told him about Francois Lake he was as interested in it as I was.

That night after our evening service some of us went out for coffee and pie, including Ivan. As we were all looking at our menus I noticed that pumpkin pie was being offered. Pumpkin pie is one of my favourites, and I said, "I know I really shouldn't, but I'm going to have a piece of this pie."

Ivan looked at me and responded, "Yes, you could lose some weight."

I found it oddly refreshing to have someone who wasn't afraid to tell the truth.

Back at my house we visited until the early hours of the morning, ending our time together with prayer. Ivan invited us all out to dinner the next evening, and once again we ended up at my place, where Ivan and I stayed up late again just talking.

At the end of our third late night together we knew we were going to get married. We prayed together, and I told Ivan that the Lord was first and foremost in my life. Everything and everybody would have to take second place to him.

I loved Ivan's honesty; what you saw was what he was—no false faces, no manipulation, just a very upright man.

Ivan went back home to William's Lake, and the following evenings we spent talking on the phone. When we each received our phone bills, totalling over $800, we knew we had to shorten our calls.

With plans now to marry, I had to phone the people in Montreal who were expecting me in just a few short weeks to interview for the music ministry position. My old counsellor gave me his blessing with a gentle coaxing for us to get premarital counselling. Ivan and I agreed that this would be a good idea.

Instead of going to Montreal to see about a job, I now went to B.C. I met Ivan there, and we drove to Francois Lake. On the way Ivan pulled off the road and asked me formally to marry him. I was incredibly thrilled to answer with a resounding "Yes!"

We continued on, picking up my niece and her husband on the way, and drove as far as we could to my property. We had to walk the last mile. It felt strange to be back there, with all that had gone on since I had lived there, but the worst part was finding that someone had broken in and stolen everything. To make matters even more heart-wrenching, the thieves had left the door open, and several animals had added their own measure of damage. Ivan saw how difficult it was for me and gave me space and time to grieve the end of that dream.

Back in Burns Lake Ivan bought an engagement ring for me, and we decided that we would be married at the end of July.

I really wanted to clean up my debt before getting married, and it only made sense to sell the property at Francois Lake. As much as we would have loved to live or at least visit there, it just wasn't practical, with no road in, no electricity, and no work for Ivan. It didn't take long to find a buyer, and the money from the sale paid off the last of my debts.

And so things moved forward towards our wedding day. We got premarital counselling and learned vital skills that would help us communicate in our relationship, avoiding mistakes that we had both made in our previous marriages.

On July 28, 1984, Ivan and I were married in an old historical church in Edmonton. The setting was beautiful. I had a moment of fear just before walking down the aisle, wondering what I was doing marrying a man I had only known for four months, but one look at Ivan set my spirit at rest.

When we put the Lord first, he will not let us go too far wrong.

EPILOGUE

For God so greatly loved and dearly prized the world
that He [even] gave up His only begotten (unique) Son,
so that whoever believes in (trusts in, clings to, relies on)
Him shall not perish (come to destruction, be lost)
but have eternal (everlasting) life.
John 3:16

Close to thirty years have passed since that wedding day. We've stood together as we've faced heart surgeries, hip replacements, breast cancer, and the death of dear family members. It hasn't been an easy journey, but easy is not a promise God gives us. He simply promises us strength for each day.

We were still on our honeymoon a few nights after our wedding, and I couldn't sleep. My spirit was bothered, and I realized I had not spent any time with the Lord since we had been married.

After a few hours of tossing and turning, I woke Ivan up and asked if we could talk. We got up, dressed, and went for a walk. I was very relieved when he agreed that if the Lord was going to be the head of our home, then we must spend time with him. We decided right then that every morning after breakfast we would read the Scriptures, share a devotion, and pray together.

That decision was life-changing. For close to thirty years we have followed that practice, and it has strengthened our marriage, giving us tremendous peace and the strength to face the trials.

I have written about my relationship with my father and how he resented me from the moment I was conceived but even more so when I was born a girl. There was never any sign from my earthly father that he loved me, and he died determined to show me his disapproval. As a result I have struggled greatly in seeing God as my heavenly Father. I know he loves me, but the journey to see him as my Father has been difficult.

Seventy-five years after my father begrudgingly took my mother to the hospital during harvesting to deliver me, God gave me complete healing through understanding a little more of my father's life and how he saw his role here. God also gave me the ability to finally forgive my earthly father. I can now call God my Father; in fact, I can call him Daddy.

The love of God for me is so great that I need to share with you how to freely receive it for yourself. You see, God loved the world so much that sent his only Son, Jesus, to redeem it. God is almighty, so much more than our minds can comprehend. He is all righteous, all merciful, and all just. We are his creation, and nothing we could possibly do after we sinned would satisfy his justice. The chasm between God and his creation is so huge that man can never reach across by his own efforts. God had to reach down his hand and pull us up, and he loves us so much that he did just that.

If you do not know my Saviour as your personal saviour, there is no better time than now. Just confess that you are a sinner, as we all are, and ask him to forgive those sins and come and live in your heart. He will live with you and care for you.

As you have no doubt learned from my story, following God doesn't necessary mean everything will be perfect, but whatever hardships you encounter, he will be with you and help you through.

Believe me, Jesus is right there whenever you call on him.

Pictures

My first attempt at running away. I was three years old and all my dolls with me.

At four years old, I was so proud of my long white stockings and new dress.

This was taken on the occasion of my first communion.

My mother and I during my boarding school days, 1950.

Family picture taken in 1943.
Back row, left to right: Pete, Hubert, George, Mike.
Middle row: Anne, Mary, Magdalene, Julia, Emma.
Front row: Me, Dad, Mom, Ray.

*Me when I was Sister Michael with my family on the occasion
of Mom and Dad's 50th wedding anniversary, 1960.
They all came to the convent to have this picture taken.*

*My sister Ann (left of me, the nun) came to visit me at the convent.
Mom and Dad also posed for this photo.*

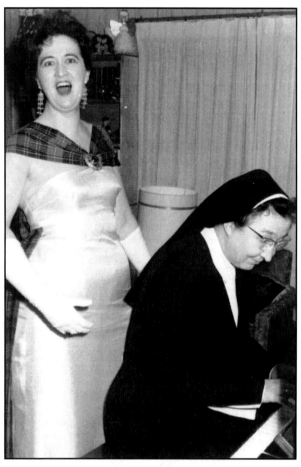

Here I am with Mother Mary Herman during one of her visits while I lived in Victoria. She was helping me practice for a Robby Burns concert.